T0151019

Riches in Real Estate

Jarett B. Shaffer&Susan S. Shaffer

Riches
in Real Estate

Have, Be, and
Do Everything
You Want

NEW YORK

LONDON • NASHVILLE • MELBOURNE • VANCOUVER

Riches in Real Estate

Have, Be, and Do Everything You Want

Published in New York, New York, by Morgan James Publishing in partnership with Difference Press. Morgan James is a trademark of Morgan James, LLC. www.MorganJamesPublishing.com

ISBN 9781642793413 paperback
ISBN 9781642793420 eBook
ISBN 9781642794403 audiobook
Library of Congress Control Number: 2018913202

Cover Design by:
Megan Dillon
megan@creativeninjadesigns.com

Interior Design by:
Christopher Kirk
www.GFSstudio.com

Cover Photo by:
Bonnie Rauch, BonsEye Photos,
www.bonseyephotos.com

Morgan James is a proud partner of Habitat for Humanity Peninsula and Greater Williamsburg. Partners in building since 2006.

Get involved today! Visit
MorganJamesPublishing.com/giving-back

Table of Contents

Foreword

J arett and Susan Shaffer are strong supporters of the Napoleon Hill Foundation. In fact, the principles taught by Napoleon Hill have greatly influenced their lives, real estate business —and the book you now hold in your hands. Inside you will find their personal stories, along with the stories of those they have helped. Their success proves that those that come from a humble background can rise up and achieve great personal and financial victories, with faith, diligence and perseverance.

Jarett learned desire as a little boy in the cold, snowy winters of Toledo, Ohio. His Grandpa Jack and Grandma Helen were good, kind people who worked hard, but they were poor. They had no running water and no indoor plumbing. Those cold trips to the bathroom in the dead of winter cultivated within him a strong desire to escape the trap of poverty and to yearn, long for, and crave success.

And, when Jarett and Susan got married and stationed in Norfolk, Virginia, they arrived in town with a baby, all their belongings in the trunk of their car, and only $78.00 to their name. They sat in a 7-Eleven parking lot and cried. After drying their tears, they set about creating their first set of goals. From that day forward, they fanned that strong desire for a successful family life and a lucrative financial career.

They got their first glimpse of success and made their first million by the age of thirty years old. And, when Jarett's Grandfather came to visit them in Chesapeake, Virginia, not only did they have running water and indoor plumbing, he chuckled and told them how proud he was of their success.

Jarett and Susan learned early on that real estate can be a labor of love. It's a field where a person can earn a tremendous amount of financial wealth and be their own boss. And along the way they learned how to create a proven roadmap to success. In this book, they spread out that map on the table and show you how you can choose to get from your current location to your chosen destination, which is presumably real estate success.

They also share straightforward strategies that they learned the hard way. This book is full of the key elements they learned. Its designed to help you to overcome fears and obstacles, both real and imaginary.

If you earnestly desire a rich fulfilling personal life and a prosperous real estate career this book can teach you how to create and build the life of your dreams—and it is a must read for you.

Don Green
Executive Director, The Napoleon Hill Foundation

Introduction

"No, no! The adventures first, explanations take such a dreadful time."
– Lewis Carroll, *Alice in Wonderland*

My guess is you absolutely know in your gut that real estate sales is your destiny. And, you are still probably trying to rekindle that initial spark you felt when you first decided to get your real estate license. Remember that feeling of excitement? It was exhilarating, right?

Every agent who gets their license dreams of the freedom from the grind of the 9-5 routine and a six-figure income. And, something in you knows that you absolutely, positively can hit real estate superstardom. But, the sad reality is that the attrition rate is high in the real estate industry. Many take off like a rocket but fall from the sky quickly and hit the ground – hard. In fact, many agents try many different strategies, they join brands that promise instant income overnight, and overlook the fact that

60-80% of what they earn is retained by their company. Some branch out on their own and try to find success buying internet leads – but have found the market is super saturated and the same leads are being sold to as many as 20-30 different agents or agencies and most of them only include an email address.

So, how do some agents make it and others don't? What's the secret? There are lots of obstacles and roadblocks, but here's what my background tells me: You picked up my book because you are destined to achieve great success in real estate and it's not a coincidence that you are reading this now. You could consider it your divine appointment with destiny. If you read this book and apply the principles inside, you will know everything you need to do to achieve your goals. You have invested too much and tried too hard to quit now. You deserve to have your big dream, and I have designed a system to help you obtain all your hopes and dreams come true. It's called *The Shaffer Way: 7 Steps to Health, Wealth, and Personal Happiness.*

So, I did my first dream board. "What would you do," the instructor asked, "if there were no barriers to stop you? If money or education wasn't an issue, what would your dream look like?" That's when I first dared to dream of being something more than I was. And I cut out pictures of a house on a sandy beach, that place by the bay I had always dreamed of having someday. I put a price tag on that, figured out what I would need to earn, and what it would take to earn it. That dream board became the image in my mind, the thing that got me up and ready to go to work each day. That was when I got my first glimpse of my future to come. I created short-term, mid-range, and long-term goals. Since that day, I have invested over a million dollars in training, coaching, workshops, seminars, one-on-one executive and business coaching, certifications, and degrees. It's unlikely I will ever stop investing in myself and growing and developing my skills. My coaches have helped me to hone my skills and have been invaluable to my success.

Along the way, I found my chosen profession: the real estate business. In my best year ever, I deposited $1.2 million into my personal household checkbook, so I am here to assure you it's totally attainable. And, you can do it too!

So, here's a fact – real estate can be a labor of love. It's a field where a person can earn a tremendous amount of financial wealth and be their own boss with limited training and very little education. It comes without the headaches of running a large firm or the troubles of investing in the considerable resources and systems and business planning that are needed in setting up even a small business. Real estate is still a small business but it can be a controlled business that only needs a few practical systems and habits and business practices that will turn into a wealth-building machine.

That's where the secrets that I have discovered over the years can help. In *The Shaffer Way: 7 Steps to Health, Wealth & Personal Happiness*, S is for Systems, H is for Happiness, A is for Antidotes, F is for Focus, F is for Finance, E is for Execution and R is for Rewards. *The Shaffer Way* is designed to empower agents to set up simple systems, turn them into habits, allow them the freedom to dominate their own lives and circumstances, get whatever their heart yearns for in terms of accomplishments, and help them raise a family, send children to college, plan for a tremendous retirement, buy whatever do-dads their hearts desire, travel the world, fund a charity, build a home – you get the picture. Step One is all about creating Systems for your real estate business. Step Two covers how to obtain true Happiness, Step Three details the Antidotes to common fears and failures, Step Four helps you to cultivate Focus, Step Five is all about the ABCs of Real Estate Math and it's super easy, Step Six is all about Execution and getting it done and Step Seven is focused on the Rewards. You will learn how to be your own boss, have no one to answer to, no hours that are set, no schedule that you have to follow. You will learn the keys to success and how to have the life that you always dreamed about and accomplish anything your heart desires. I have learned many secrets over the last 30 years and I am excited and honored to share them with you.

Agents that turn their passions into habits can become tremendously powerful in their target market area. It's a little-known fact that most real estate agents have a license and don't even sell one house each year. In fact, over 50% of the market in which I work is made up of agents that have not sold a home in over a year. That is a tremendously expensive hobby. It costs a great deal to keep a real estate license and access to the multiple listing service if you aren't going to be serious about selling homes. I am guessing that if you have this book and you are reading it, that you didn't spend all that time and money getting into real estate to make it a hobby. There's good news. This proven system – The Shaffer Way – will help you plan and structure your real estate career in a way that assures success, whether the market is headed for the stratosphere or threatening to circle the drain.

Real estate is special in that way. If it sounds too good to be true – it's really not. You can have your cake and eat it too. It's one of the few careers you can choose where your upbringing or your lack of formal education doesn't predict your success. You can break free – if you dare to dream. You just need a proven roadmap. In this book, I am spreading out that map on the table, showing you how you can choose to get from your current location to your chosen destination. In the chapters to come, I help you to examine various routes and create your own real estate GPS. You were born to be a real estate superstar – so let's get started!

Chapter One:

Why

"Why it's simply impassible!
Alice: Why, don't you mean impossible?
Door: No, I do mean impassible. (chuckles)
Nothing's impossible!"
– Lewis Carroll, *Alice's Adventures in Wonderland*
& Through the Looking-Glass

You can't spend more than three decades in close contact with agents and not appreciate this singular truth: agents are always looking for the best advice and the fastest fixes to improve their business. And, I know that you picked up this book because you aren't complacent. Like most agents, you probably started out with a traditional compensation package at a brokerage with traditional commission splits, based on production performance and fees for technology, marketing, errors and omissions insurance, desk fees, office fees, etc. Most of those places have annual reviews that revolve around the broker discussing how much the company can pay or not pay, without a hint of how they intend to give back – or to empower you to grow to your individual earning potential. This well-established model usually assumes that increased production is the result of traditional forms of training. Most agents are lured to agencies that practice the employee model with a promise of super star achievement. But that glosses over the reality of low commission splits and expensive, time-consuming technical training that does nothing to help drive your personal household income. That's probably where you are right now.

To be fair, some companies do hold classes and seminars that give away a couple of nuggets that resonate with listeners and encourage feelings of success. "Anyone can do it," agents are told. But the underlying message is that if you're really serious about building your client roster and signing more sales agreements, you'll be willing to write checks over and over again to get – or try to get – the necessary knowledge. And then, agents without the resources or inclination to do so will be treated as unserious. The result? Intra-office jealousies, an atmosphere of haves and have nots, free-floating resentment, and sometimes barely concealed hostility. And it's all based on a lie! The sad reality is that you and the majority of the agents who shell out the big bucks for these seminars and classes aren't much better off than they were before the training. And all those leads that they promised, well, they don't amount to much more than a bunch of email addresses that you could have gotten on your own.

Now you are stuck with a really unfair split and a bunch of other agents who can't or don't execute any better than the ones who couldn't or didn't pay for training. And you are asking yourself how you got lumped in with a bunch of chickens? You know you deserve to fly with the eagles. Why are you scratching and pecking on the floor with the others when you deserve to fly? You instinctively know the training they are providing doesn't focus on the right systems and skills needed to grow you to your potential and that those leads are just a bunch of trash. And, you have come to realize that the training just focuses exclusively on building the company and its brand and its products.

Obstacles to Success

There's a reason for this generalized lack of success in most realty offices. None of the brokers are mentoring and coaching. Often, the reason is because the broker in charge doesn't know how and they have never been coached. In fact, the person promoted to leadership in the office is usually the superstar performer – the person who may have the most sales experience, but perhaps little or no expertise in training up the next crop of high performing agents. The skill of the typical broker-turned-manager is limited to selling and climbing the ladder and most have been, á la the Peter Principle, promoted to their level of incompetence. And, instead of a servant leader, you get stuck with a manager determined to spread success by intimidation and fear. Many of these big-ego bosses expect unquestioning followers. For the average agent, it's simply sink or swim.

Added Frustrations

Then there are the promised leads used to lure unsuspecting agents to their current office. Once there and producing, they learn the leads that are handed out are nothing more than an email address and a fruitless attempt to contact a real buyer or seller in the hopes of gaining clients. And, you have probably realized that the good leads are only given to the one or two favorites in the office and they are closely held and jealously guarded. It's just simply disheartening and sad.

Plenty of realty groups will tell you that they exist to do well by doing good, but the real message is sell sell sell. And if you don't figure out how to sell sell sell, they will want you to go go go.

Then, there are internet leads companies calling you constantly trying to sell you more and more marketing systems, but they don't promise to deliver and when questioned about their success rate or challenged for money back guarantees, the sales rep can't get off the phone with you fast enough. The Zillows of the world promise agents an easy recipe for growing their business: wait 'til a buyer clicks on their face, sends them an email, or calls them up out of the blue. A set-it-and-forget-it model of attracting new clients, what could be better? Indeed, what could be better? How about knowing in advance that they sell those leads to 20-30 other agents for the exact same price in the exact same area as you? How about not missing dinner with your kids or their soccer game because you have to go meet the prospect at the property in hopes of securing them as a client? The specter looms over you and you know if you don't trade your precious family time, you worry that one of the 20-30 will and then, you will be down one more sale. In your gut, you know you shouldn't, but you make the trade to leave the game and meet the potential buyer. Then the online lead, which came easily, easily goes. Buyers are fickle, and without any personal connection to their agent, they're more likely to move along to that next agent, that next home without much thought. Agents find themselves frantically trying to catch leads the moment they come through, and then entertain them well enough that they will consider signing that elusive exclusivity agreement. And now, you are placed firmly on the hamster wheel with no way to get off.

What's often overlooked is teaching you how to cultivate the relationship. Last year, 70–80% of all real estate transactions originated from an existing relationship with an agent.

And those billions of dollars in leads? Did you know that they only accounted for 12% of all transactions? Buyers start looking online before they purchase and they interact with many different agents during that process. It's usually 18 to 24 months before they finally make a purchase decision. At any point in that process, they might end up going with another agent. But here's the frustrating truth: 7 out of 10 people usually work with the first agent they interact with when they are getting ready to move. Staying top of mind is important. But being there at the right time is essential.

Some days, it seems like the internet leads have won. But a few years from now, we'll be telling a different story – your story.

What separates the successful from the unsuccessful isn't their willingness to invest in their careers or whether they care enough to grow their skills. You are here reading this because you know you need to throw off the ropes of those traditional mindsets, get off the proverbial hamster wheel, and learn real systems that work, steps that provide wealth and empower you to achieve your dreams and desires. You need something instead of your management harassing you and nagging you and driving you to sell more and more for the betterment of the agency – nibbling away at your profit at your expense. And there's more to your story because you have the power to write it. Together, we are going to discover what is your big why and the type of real estate sales that you can pursue with passion. We are going to uncover your hidden talents and teach you how to wield your skills and give you the tools to turn you into a master real estate sales artist. We will examine if your big why is in alignment with your dreams. You will get a lens through which to examine what you need to do to create a more successful entrepreneurial mindset. You will learn some of the first course corrections you'll need to make and how. I will give you the tools you need to get there and you will learn all about what's holding you back and how to break free and re-write your own destiny – your way. You will learn why most real estate agents flounder and fail, and it's not because they're lacking intelligence, ambition, or energy. My goal is to share with you an inspirational, how-to model with instructions and help you achieve your goals and your dreams. So let's get out the map and plot out this trip together!

Chapter Two:

Desire

> "Alice: Would you tell me, please,
> which way I ought to go from here?
> The Cheshire Cat: That depends a good deal on
> where you want to get to.
> Alice: I don't much care where.
> The Cheshire Cat: Then it doesn't much matter
> which way you go.
> Alice:...So long as I get somewhere.
> The Cheshire Cat: Oh, you're sure to do that,
> if only you walk long enough."
> – Lewis Carroll, *Alice in Wonderland*

Desire – when you look up the definition, it speaks of craving, longing, strongly wanting to have or obtain something. My guess is that's why you are here: to learn what to do so you can get what you want. And success is right around the corner for you. You can transform your life, your work, your wealth, and your circumstances, no matter what you have experienced in the past. It doesn't matter what has held you back, what obstacle you have faced, or who has stood in your way.

You see, I learned desire as a little boy in the cold, snowy winters of Toledo, Ohio. I used to go and stay with my grandparents very often. My Grandpa Jack and Grandma Helen were good, kind people who worked hard, but they were poor. They had no running water and no indoor plumbing. As children, we innocently think everyone else's reality is just like ours. So, I thought everyone had grandparents who were poor, just like mine. At their house, when it was the middle of the night and you had to go to the bathroom, you had to venture out into the cold and use the outhouse. I still remember the cold of that toilet seat and the care to make certain that I didn't get stuck to it.

So, I can honestly tell you, I had a strong desire to escape the trap of poverty and those experiences taught me to yearn, long for, and crave success. It burned in my heart and my mind and I was determined to escape poverty. I got my first glimpse of success when I set my mind to make my first million by the age of thirty years old and I did, just before my thirty-first birthday. And, when my Grandfather came to visit me in my home in Chesapeake, Virginia, not only did I have running water and indoor plumbing, he chuckled and told me I did not have a home, that I lived in a hotel. I was proud to show him what I had achieved and glad he was able to see my accomplishments.

I broke free, and you can too. Today is the first day of the rest of your life and you are about to have a giant breakthrough. And, it's not a fairy tale. There are many others that have gone ahead and we are going to examine their paths, learn how they did it, and, together, we are going to forge ahead into the exciting new destiny that awaits you.

Henry's Story

All it takes is desire, that earnest craving to be, do, and have everything you want. One of my clients started working with me a little over three years ago. His name is changed to maintain his privacy, but he told me that I could share his story. I will call him Henry. Henry faced great adversity as a young person and was raised in poverty. He only had two outfits to wear and each day, had to have one washed so he could wear the other the next day. He had a career in the United States Military and completed an honorable retirement there. After serving in the military, he decided to start his second career in the real estate and mortgage banking industry. And three years ago, Henry and I started working together. In the first twelve months of working together, he experienced the highest production of real estate sales he had accomplished in his entire real estate career – and he had just turned 80 years old. Success has no age limits and faces no boundaries. He is now 82 and following the principles I outline in *The Shaffer Way*. In fact, this year, Henry is on target to generate over fifteen million dollars in additional sales production and just wrapped up several million dollars in the last thirty days. If you are reading this and were concerned that your time for experiencing success has already passed you by, consider Henry's story.

In fact, your story is unfolding right now, before your very eyes and – with this set of directions – you will be on the real estate highway to success. Real estate success doesn't require hard labor and it doesn't require a great deal of education. All it takes is imagination and desire. If you can visualize riches in your imagination and desire them in your heart, you can gain them in your bank balance. As long as you have firmly in your mind what you want – you can possess it.

Financial Riches of Your Own Choosing

You can have financial riches based on your goals and desires. If you serve others and you have faith in your goals and objectives, you can do it. And, you don't have to listen to anyone or anything that says you can't. You can rise above your present circumstances, capture your dreams, and have the financial wealth of your own choice, when you want and where you want. You only have to begin to think, "What do I want most – is it money, fame, power, peace of mind, happiness?" Maybe it's a combination of all of these.

Freedom from Anxiety and Fear

You can have freedom from anxiety and fear. I am going to share with you that fear is also a state of mind and that you don't have to live with it or suffer from it. You can throw off the mindset that has kept you from achieving your hopes and, in fact, may have kept you from even attempting to dream your big dream. Later in the book, I will outline the six basic fears that all men and women suffer from and how you can be free from them all. In easy, breezy techniques, you will transform into a master gardener and be able to root out the insidious and subtle lies that have crept into the beautiful landscape of your mind. Together, we will apply the right combination of weed killers and cultivate a lush garden.

Inner Peace and a Quiet Mind

There is a parable about peace of mind that I would like to share. A woman whose husband died unexpectedly faced dire circumstances. Creditors hounded her, taking everything away from her and her young son. Fearing she might lose the most valuable possession of the family, she hid the priceless jewel that had been handed down for generations by sowing it into the sleeve of an old coat that the creditors would never want. The troubles weighed on her grief and eventually broke her spirit and she died without ever telling her son about the jewel.

The boy found himself without family or home and his only inheritance the old threadbare coat that the creditors left him. He found work wherever he could, staying in barns or out in the forest, exposed to the elements and grave hardship. Filled with sorrow at his fate, he endured the passing years with an abiding belief in the unfairness of life.

One day, as he was chopping wood, his sleeve caught on a branch and tore open. Out spilled the priceless jewel onto the ground before him!

The point is, we were born rich, and with peace of mind – we only need to cultivate it. It just seems elusive when experiencing feelings of deprivation. This is because, of course, the jewel represents the perfect nature of the true, original self with which all of us are born. Upon finding the jewel, the young man realized he had been rich all along – and his life changed irreversibly. This book will help you to become more aware of the hidden jewel you carry and to bring you in touch with the source of inner peace and happiness. The more you can learn to identify with your own hidden treasure, the more you will learn to truly have peace of mind.

Joyful Work

You deserve work that you can enjoy doing and which brings forth your very best creative expression. I think that's why you chose real estate in the first place. It's natural to earnestly yearn for freedom of body and mind. Who wants to be the person that waits in line at the same traffic light, day in, day out at the same time, taking the same route to work, listening to the same music or news, drinking the same coffee, and experiencing torment and boredom. Instead, the real estate muse called to you and you heard her siren song – and answered. To have a labor of love is to have one of the great riches in life and you can unlock the mysteries of this kind of love. Won't it feel great to lay your head on your pillow at night with your heart full of joy, and your mind filled with eager thoughts about tomorrow and what comes next! With those sweet thoughts, you can experience sweet slumber and sound health.

A Box of Rewards or Punishments

You see, at birth each of us receives two different boxes. One is labeled "Rewards," and the other is marked, "Punishments." In the first box is a list of the benefits we may enjoy and it contains all the things we desire in this life. In the second is a list of the consequences we must face. In this book, we will break the seal on those two packages and examine their contents. In the following chapters, I plan to share with you what I have discovered after analyzing the success of many hundreds of men and women. You will see that they all had certain things in common and habits they developed which helped them to achieve great success. There is a certain roadmap to follow with milestones, metrics, and methods for arriving at your desired destination. If you follow the plan developed and outlined here – and do so fervently and persistently – you will be able to be, do, and have anything your heart desires.

Chapter Three:

Plan

> *"'Who are **you**?' said the Caterpillar.*
> *This was not an encouraging opening for a conversation.*
> *Alice replied, rather shyly, 'I – I hardly know, sir, just at*
> *present – at least I know who I WAS when I got up this*
> *morning, but I think I must have been changed several*
> *times since then.'"*
> — Lewis Carroll, *Alice in Wonderland*

In Chapter Two, we embarked upon the exercise to examine your desires to help you discover – or rediscover – the things that matter to you most. Although it's entertaining to listen to the banter between Alice and the Caterpillar – it's not so funny when it becomes a dose of reality and a revelation of our current state of circumstances. So, we begin this internal examination by asking, "Why am I doing this? Why did I choose this? Where is this coming from?" These are actual conversations you are having with yourself all the time. Even if you don't realize it, it's taking place in your subconscious mind. As we begin to bring this internal dialogue into the realm of the conscious mind, well, in the beginning, you may not like the answers. In fact, you may find that you wouldn't let anyone else talk to you the way you are talking to yourself – but, more on that in later chapters.

Once you answer these questions, you won't have to spend so much time analyzing and wringing your hands over what to do next. I am here to help! In the remaining chapters, you'll begin to learn how it feels naturally when all is moving in the right direction and how to use your intuition more. You'll find answers start coming to you more readily and, instead of exhausting yourself chasing them like squirrels or rabbits, they manifest the best possible solutions, to your very obvious delight.

Internal Examination and Introspection

Let's begin an internal examination and begin to draw your own personal journey out on the table. Some questions will follow and I encourage you to grab your journal or a piece of paper and write out these answers. As you do so, start with what is right there, on the tip of your tongue, waiting to be expressed. Try not to edit yourself. Let everything that's there come out. Keep a "wide" view: think about all aspects of your life and not just about your business.

- What really matters to you in life and who do you want to share it with?
- When do you feel the most alive?
- What do you want your life to look and feel like?
- What do you value most?
- What's important to you?
- What are the most important things you want to focus on in this current phase of your life?
- How do you want your life to feel on a day-to-day basis?
- What feelings would you have if you were "in your groove" throughout the day?
- Do you spend time during your day thinking about what could be?
- Is there a moment during the day that makes you feel as though someone hit the pause button?
- What are the pictures and feelings that come up over and over again of your heart's desires?
- Of all the things you've experienced in your life, what about real estate has given you the most satisfaction or pleasure? This one sounds easy, but it isn't always easy to pinpoint what absolutely exhilarates you. What is it?
- Is there something that you used to do that gave you a feeling that you wish you could recapture and can

you visualize yourself recreating that feeling in the real estate world?

- What gets you completely engaged in real estate, and moves you to exceed everyone's expectations, including your own? What's the feeling of that experience?
- What are your greatest strengths in real estate? Is it listings, is it buyers, is it working with investors, is it commercial property, is it property management, is it investment property, is it staging homes?

As you analyze the answers, see if you notice any patterns that have begun to emerge. The answers to these questions provide an opportunity to evaluate what is having an impact on your real estate business in counterproductive ways. I can virtually guarantee that there's a substantial gap between how you want your business to operate and how it actually is operating day to day. The gift you're giving yourself by beginning to do this work, is to change that. The real work is to figure out why or how you don't actually value what you thought you did, and then do something about it. Again, this is not about self-blame. And, it's not about being perfect either.

Failing Forward – Learning from the Past

It's possible that you uncovered some truly enlightening pieces of information that have given you some clues as to why you are having difficulties achieving the real estate success you were born to experience. It's what we do with the information now that counts. You may conclude that you have experienced difficulties and some defeats. In the words of Dr. Napoleon Hill, from the Science of Success Philosophy, "While the circumstances of life are such that everyone must undergo a certain amount of temporary defeat, you can find hope in the knowledge that every such defeat carries with it the seed of an equivalent or a greater benefit." The great poet, Emerson, said that our strength grows out of our struggle. It's the seed of benefit that must be cultivated and found when sorting through defeats. When we are pushed, tormented, and poked, we have to develop our wits, our stamina, develop personal initiative, self-determination, and perseverance. It's the setbacks, trials and tribulations that help us to develop these muscles and these skills. It's then that we can begin to cultivate an attitude of gratitude and begin to thank our circumstances, embrace our faults, and recognize that they are the teachers of our greatest endeavors, yet to come.

You may have encountered great struggles, experienced loss, defeat, and suffered greatly. There may have been circumstances which were unavoidable or out of your control. Honest, heartfelt answers to the questions above allow you to begin to design a new roadmap to a new destination, complete with the by-passes and cloverleafs necessary to avoid life's traffic jams. A person's courage shows up when faced with adversity. Real courage is found when it's hard to get out of bed in the morning, or to pick up the phone and call a client when something went sideways, or to take personal responsibility when it's yours to own. Courage is something we all have and we can tap into it at any time – we just have to decide to.

Empowering Transformation – The Road to Change

When you woke up this morning, your brain went to work to spend the rest of the day trying to protect you and to make sure you will survive. In fact, your primitive brain is still on high alert when you walk out the front door every morning. It's scanning the horizon for Tyrannosaurs and Velociraptors, trying to keep you alive. And, it wants to keep everything exactly the same as the day before – because it knows that everything you did yesterday is OK, because you didn't die. You woke up this morning, so the brain thinks, OK let's repeat those exact same set of circumstances, because if we do that, we won't die. So, you aren't crazy, there's a very good reason you feel resistant to change. It's because your brain thinks change is deadly. But we know in our rational mind, change is necessary if we want things to – well – change, right?

Let's examine the science. Resistance to change often manifests itself as feelings of fear and anxiety. We experience the feeling of dread in contemplating change. It's that icky feeling that something bad is going to happen, we just don't know what the bad is. A major factor in how we experience fear has to do with the context. When our "thinking" brain gives feedback to our "emotional" brain and we perceive ourselves as being in a safe space, we can then quickly shift the way we experience that high arousal state, going from one of fear to one of enjoyment or excitement. Fear reaction starts in the brain and spreads through the body to make adjustments for the best defense. The fear response starts in a region of the brain called the amygdala. This almond-shaped set of nuclei in the temporal lobe of the brain is dedicated to detecting the emotional salience of the stimuli – how much something stands out to us. This leads to bodily changes that prepare us to be more efficient in a danger: The brain becomes hyperalert, pupils dilate, the bronchi dilate, and breathing accelerates. Heart rate and blood pressure rise. Blood flow and the stream of glucose to the skeletal muscles increase. Organs not vital in survival, such as the gastrointestinal system, slow down. In simple terms, you begin to breathe fast, your forehead and palms get sweaty, your stomach feels tight, and you just plain want to run for the hills.

It's all about perspective. For instance, seeing a lion in the wild can trigger a strong fear reaction, but the response to a view of the same lion at a zoo is more of curiosity and thinking that the lion is cute. This is because the hippocampus and the frontal cortex process contextual information, and inhibitory pathways dampen the amygdala fear response and its down-stream results. Basically, our "thinking" circuitry of brain reassures our "emotional" areas that we are, in fact, OK. With this science in our back pocket, the next time you experience the emotions of fear and anxiety, pat your pocket, it's right there, and tell yourself – out loud – "I am excited!" It will tell your brain everything's OK and your body will return to its normal state of being. The panic will subside and you can continue the path toward change.

Pamela's Story

Prior to working with me, Pamela had experienced large surges of anxiety about changing the way she approached her real estate career. Each day, she felt trapped on the hamster wheel and compelled to capitulate to the whims and desires of her clients, whatever and whenever they wanted her attention. This led to interruptions in her home life and greater levels of anxiety and sometimes full-blown panic attacks. Her constant fear was that if she didn't drop whatever she was doing, she would lose her clients, or they wouldn't refer her to family and friends. Within twelve months of working together, Pamela was able to take off an entire day, without answering her phone. No crisis happened and she didn't lose a single client. After instituting the systems found in *The Shaffer Way*, she not only stopped having panic attacks, she decreased her working hours by 15 hours per week and doubled her business and her income.

Excitement – Not Fear

Now, we can discuss change in the right context and embrace it as "excitement" – not fear. Isn't it wonderful that you get to live the rest of your life in a state of excitement, free from the traps of fear and worry? In simple terms – to change our circumstances, we have to change how we think. It really is that simple and I am here to show you how.

What's Next

We are going to spend the rest of the book learning how to change our circumstances by changing how we think. It begins with viewing all of life through a positive mental attitude. Earlier we discussed those two boxes – one marked "Rewards" and one marked "Punishments." A positive mind will find a way that things can be done; however, a negative one looks for all the reasons it can't be done. In the next chapter, we will break the seal and begin to examine the contents of the two packages through *The Shaffer Way: 7 Steps to Health, Wealth & Personal Happiness*.

Always know – I am here to help! To set up a call with me, just email me at jarettshaffer@gmail.com and someone on my team will hook you up with an appointment on my calendar.

Chapter Four:

Step One – Systems

*"You know what the issue is with this world? Everyone
wants some magical solution to their problem and
everyone refuses to believe in magic."*
– The Mad Hatter, *Alice in Wonderland*

S ystems are the new sexy – alluring, appealing, fulfilling,
deeply satisfying and with a giant payout when performed
with skill.

And, you won't need magic to achieve your dream come
true; once these systems are in full swing, it will feel as though
someone sprinkled the pixie dust of success all over your world.

You have heard the old adage that the definition of insanity
is to continue doing the same thing and expecting a different
result. In this chapter, you will learn to create the changes you
desire – the secrets necessary to achieve health, wealth, and personal happiness.

The Box Marked Riches

Let's get started by breaking the seal on those proverbial packages and discussing what's inside. The box marked riches includes sound health, peace of mind, a labor of love, freedom from fear and worry, a positive mental attitude, and material riches of your own choice and quantity. As discussed earlier, each one of us is given the opportunity to choose which of the boxes we wish to direct our minds toward.

The Box Marked Punishments

Unfortunately, if we neglect to cultivate the opportunities presented in the package marked riches, we will inherit the box marked punishments by default. The box marked punishments contains poverty and lack, mental and physical ailments of all kinds, fear and worry, a negative mental attitude, a job you hate, and a wasted life.

Which One Will You Choose?

Many blessings are achieved by focusing upon riches, and all achievement starts with knowing what you want. The previous exercises were helpful in determining what you want, which presumably is success. The key involves keeping your mind keenly focused on the things that you want and off of the things that you do not want. In other words, success attracts more success and failure attracts more failure. If you want to be successful, you have to fix your mind on the positive thoughts and focus on them with all your heart and mind. We will cover how to cultivate gratitude later in the book. That practice alone can help you to fix your internal gaze upon the object of your desire. When you close the door of your mind to negative thoughts, the door of opportunity opens to you. A positive mental attitude is paramount and critical to achieving your goals. Think of it this way: You either ride this life, or it rides you. Your mental attitude decides who is the rider and who is the horse.

Your Definite Life Plan

A definite life plan is the starting point for the achievement of your goals in life. Failure to determine a definite life plan causes 98% of the world to drift aimlessly through life without the slightest idea of the work they are best fitted for and no concept whatsoever for the definite life objective that can be achieved. If you have the ambition to start making life pay off on your own terms, congratulations, you have come to the right place. It's important to note that successful people move on their own initiative but they know where they are going before they start. If you are ready, you will grasp these ideas and this will be the turning point of your entire life!

SYSTEM – Save Your Self Time Effort and Money

Moreover, in order to run a successful real estate career, you need effective systems and strategies that work. Systems are simply a fancy word for habits. As far as strategies go – you need two key elements. First, what you are doing needs to matter to your existing and potential customers. Second, it needs to makes you different from all the other agents – it differentiates you. Think of it this way: SYSTEM – Save Your Self Time, Effort, and Money.

How to Create a System – *The Shaffer Way* – It's Easy as 1, 2, 3

- Number One, decide what you want,
- Number two, create a plan to achieve step one, write a draft on it, keep revising your draft until your plan is sound and then,
- Number three, execute.

Natural law runs in much the same way. The stars and the planets operate with clocklike precision. Think of it: the sun comes up in the morning, and goes down at night. The ocean runs according to tides – the tide comes in and the tide goes out. The seasons operate in a rhythmical fashion. As you can predict the season to follow the one you are in, so too your business needs the benefits of these clock-like habits to run in a consistent fashion.

Habits and Order

Next you need order. Order is predictable action and reaction. All of us are ruled by our habits and they are accepted by us because of our repeated thoughts and experiences. Therefore, we can control our business to the extent that we control our thoughts. Currently, you have created patterns of thought by repeating certain ideas or behaviors and natural law takes over those patterns and makes them more or less permanent, unless you change them.

It's an awesome fact that we can control our thoughts and direct them toward a definite major purpose to achieve our goals. Three principles form the voluntary establishment of a habit. It starts with plasticity, the capability of change to be molded into the desired objective or shape. This is accomplished by the implementation of will power. Next is frequency of impression. Repetition is the mother of all learning. We can decide to be lazy and indifferent or ambitious and energetic. Make no mistake, either is a decision. Last is the intensity of the impression. Let me give a personal example. My wife and I decided we needed to change our habits as it pertains to personal health. To do so, we fixed our minds on what we wanted – sound health and long life. Then, we began to brainstorm the number of ways that we could accomplish that goal that would be consistent, systematic, and habitual. We researched best methods, consulted experts, and created a draft of a plan. We modified the plan and created new drafts until we decided upon a course of action. We then created a goal to walk two miles every day for 365 days. At first, it was very difficult and overwhelming. There were many days we just didn't feel like staying the course, but we relied upon one another for accountability. We are now in our third year of walking two miles per day every single day and have not missed a single day. That is the power of creating a system, executing a plan, and turning it into habits.

A System to Serve Based on the Ten Basic Motives

In real estate, we are in the people business. Understanding what matters most to your clients is vital to serving them. There are ten basic motives that are important to your clients and also to you. They are the desire for self-preservation, the emotion of love, the emotion of fear, the emotion of sex, the desire for life after death, the desire for freedom of body and mind, the desire for revenge, the emotion of hate, the desire for self-expression and recognition, and the desire for material gain. You will find that unless specific goals are supported with the proper number of these motives, you are not going to be motivated to carry out your plans to successful conclusion. A burning desire behind your specific goals is essential and you won't have a burning desire unless you have a motive that sets you on fire.

Now it's time to determine what it is that you desire most from life and make that your definite life purpose and goal. Close your eyes and visualize your growth; see yourself five years from now and ten years from now. Then, set up a minor purpose in six months or even a year from now that will be the stepping stones to lead you toward your definite life purpose.

The SMART System – Specific, Measurable, Accountable, Realistic, and Timebound

The goals you set need to be created using the SMART system. Each goal must be specific, measurable, accountable, realistic, and timebound. Using this framework, write out a clear, concise statement of your goal, just as if you were writing a letter to a friend, explaining what it is you really desire from life. List the benefits which will manifest, using the right combination of motives we evaluated earlier. Write out a list of the information and knowledge you will need to acquire to reach your objectives. Write down how much you desire to earn and receive each year. List the places you desire to visit and list the skills you desire to master. As you list these, write out a separate statement of the motive which prompts each desire. Combine each of your objectives with the motive necessary to propel you toward that desire. This will empower you to manifest the burning desire necessary to push you along. Each morning, read the statement of your specific goals in life aloud until you have them memorized and imprinted upon your mind so that you can call up your objectives at any given moment. Visualize the benefits you will enjoy when reaching each milestone.

The System of Developing a Pleasing Personality

What kind of a person will you need to become in order to make these dreams come true? To examine our starting point, let's conduct a check-up from the neck up and see if we detect any stinking thinking that we need to get rid of. To do so, I would like to share with you a philosopher's prayer about cultivating a pleasing personality. "Let me be open minded on all subjects so that I can grow mentally and spiritually. May the time never come when I will be above learning from the humblest person. Let me never forget that a closed mind is a narrow mind. May I never express opinions on any subject unless they are founded upon reasonably dependable knowledge. Forbid that I should ever find fault with another because he may not agree with me. May I always show a wholesome respect for those with whom I may not agree. Let me be always mindful of the fact that all my knowledge is as nothing when compared to all that remains to be learned. Give me the courage to admit my ignorance when I am asked a question about which I know little or nothing. May I always share with others such knowledge as I may possess which can be of help to them. Let me never forget that humility of heart will attract more friends than all the wisdom of mankind and let me remain ever a student in search of truth, and never pretend to be a finished scholar on any subject." – Napoleon Hill

Those attitudes lead toward a pleasing personality.

System to Discover Areas for Improvement

Let's examine the other side of that ledger to detect any areas which may need some tinkering and growth.

- Do you have the habit of interrupting when others are talking?
- Do you make suggestions using sarcasm or negative insinuations?
- Do you exaggerate or add filler for emphasis?
- Do you care more about yourself and think little of others and their interests?
- Do you use flattery to get what you want?
- Do you gossip?
- Are you critical of yourself and others?
- Are you in the habit of arguing when others disagree?
- Do you have the habit of focusing on your ills and pains?
- Are you in the habit of offering unsolicited advice to others?
- Are you open minded?

- Do you experience flairs of temper or uncontrolled anger?
- Do you try to get a discount on everything but expect others to pay you full price?

It takes genuine courage to evaluate the answers to those questions. I ask that you avoid judging yourself. Instead, become curious as to why you might have developed the above attitudes and thoughts. Have the determination to look at and examine where those patterns of thinking originated. And, there's good news – you can change your behavior by the introduction of new habits and you can start today!

Amy's Story

Prior to my working with Amy, she experienced the typical highs and lows of most real estate agents. She would have a great quarter, work really hard on generating leads and turn them into clients. For a few months, she would be flush with clients and listings and buyers. Then, since she created the clients all about the same time, the listings and the buyers would all go under contract at about the same time. Next, she worked super hard to provide outstanding customer service and got very busy coordinating all the inspections, repairs, meeting every necessary deadline, and attending to all the details. Often, she worked 80-90 hours per week during this busy time to ensure that everything went just perfectly for her clients. Right before working together, she even bought her buyers a new washer and dryer, just to sweeten the deal.

Unfortunately, the clients never sent her a referral or even a thank you card for that matter. She naturally expected that the clients would be so pleased and appreciative that when she passed out her business cards and asked for referrals at the closing table business would simply roll in the door. Then for the next quarter, she would experience the low and it would be crickets. No new listings, no new buyers, and she would become very discouraged.

She didn't realize that the key to keeping an even real estate business is running her business with systems. When we started working together, we created a plan, established functional systems, and in no time at all, she doubled her income because she no longer wasted two quarters per year wondering where the next set of clients would come from. She is much more able to keep an even schedule, work a steady 25-30 hours per week, and has experienced a ten times increase in her overall business. She is much happier and financially ahead by established systems – The Shaffer Way.

SWOT System Analysis

Now it's time to conduct a SWOT analysis of your plan. You will need to evaluate the Strengths, Weaknesses, Opportunities, and Threats involved in the attainment of your objectives. This will take personal initiative and self-discipline. First, draw out a large square and divide it into four smaller squares. Label each box, Strengths in one box, Weaknesses in the next box, Opportunities in the third box, and Threats in the next box. Brainstorm by quickly writing down as many of the items in each column as you can. Give yourself two minutes on a stopwatch or the timing feature on your phone. Be sure not to criticize; just let all the ideas pour out of you and onto the page in each area. Once you have completed the exercise, go back over each list and keep only the top three in each category. These lists will help you to evaluate the soundness of your plans and your goals.

Congratulations! You have completed Step One. Next up: Step Two – Happiness.

Can you come up with a similar plan? If it seems overwhelming, I'm here to help. Reach out to me for a private strategy session and we can map out your desired outcomes together. Email me at jarettshaffer@gmail.com to schedule an appointment to strategize.

Chapter Five:

Step Two – Happiness

"I give myself very good advice, but very seldom follow it."
– Alice, *Alice in Wonderland*

L
ike Alice, we often give ourselves great advice and then promptly decide not to follow it. It's a paradox in life: We know the thing that we should do – yet, when it comes time, we turn away, hit life's proverbial snooze button, and pull the covers back over our head – but why? The change we want to make is uncomfortable, it doesn't feel natural, and it goes against our basic instincts.

To illustrate, I want to tell you a story about my son's wrestling coach. It is often said that wrestling is 90% mental. The coach had several mantras that you could always count on hearing at each practice and at wrestling matches. First, he would tell his wrestlers, "It's not fancy pins or moves that win wrestling matches. It's the basics – and we are going to drill the basics until you can do these moves every time because you have practiced them so often they become natural. Wrestlers that try to muscle their way to a win will lose to a wrestler with better technique." That's the speech he used when the young men on the team would win a round by pulling out some unusual pin technique and overcoming their opponent using the unusual strategy. But, my favorite coaching advice was "Turn and face." In wrestling, when the opposing wrestler has you in a head lock or is close to a pin, it's a natural instinct to want to do what is called "flee the mat" or try to get away. The coach would always say the way to break free and avoid getting pinned is to go against your natural instinct and turn and face your opponent – dead on.

The Happiness of Self Discipline

You see, when you turn and face, the opposing wrestler loses the advantage. In life, our natural instinct is to flee the mat and try to get away from that person or thing that we feel is going to pin us. Instead of giving in to instinct, you need to turn and face your opponent. We achieve happiness when we try, even if we fail. Failure is an event, not a person.

We talked earlier about learning the benefits from adversity and defeat. There is always a seed of benefit from every defeat if you only look to find it. Often, upon reflection, it's the greatest difficulties that bring about the sweetest victories once we learn to truly see things as they really are. What I am really talking about is self-discipline. There are so many benefits to mental and emotional self-discipline. Here are just a few: Your imagination will become more alert, your enthusiasm will grow, you will develop greater initiative, your self-reliance will increase, you will look at the world through different eyes, your problems will mentally melt away, your personality will become more magnetic, and you will find people seeking you who had previously ignored or overlooked you. Your hopes and ambitions will be higher and stronger and your faith will become more powerful. Self-discipline is the tool with which anyone may harness and direct their inborn emotions. Self-discipline will help you win life's wrestling matches.

The Happiness in Living in the Present Moment

Take a moment and close your eyes. This moment is yours, a gift you are giving yourself. This is a moment that is all yours. Notice as you draw in your breath, simply breathe in and breathe out. Notice what you notice. Is your breath sharp and jagged or smooth and soft? Next, take a long, sweet inhale of breath, deep into your belly, now let it out slowly and gently, and feel the sweet simple joy of being alive. Now repeat that three more times.

Isn't that amazing? Could you imagine it would feel so good just to sit here and breathe? Can you simply tune into how you are feeling, right now, at this moment in time? Take this opportunity to think of all the things you love about you, your surroundings, your family, your home, this room. Take in all the beauty that surrounds you, exactly as it is right now. Allow your mind to wander following the path of those gentle thoughts. Notice that your heart is beating; give thanks for your heart. Follow the beats of your heart and notice the rhythm. Tune into this natural cycle. This is a declaration of life. Next, notice that you are able to experience your breath and feel the inhale and the exhale, notice how sweet it is when your lungs are full and how good it feels to exhale. This moment is yours; allow yourself to wallow in the pleasure of the sweetness of this space. Take a moment to meditate upon all the things you are thankful for today. This is your bliss. This is your sweet and special place in your mind where you can return to at any time. Take this moment to feel completely happy and know that this wonderful state of being is available to you at any time you want to return to this state of feeling. Can you make this a morning routine? Can you decide right now to let this be the way you spend the first ten minutes of every day, sitting in a quiet space, meditating upon all that is good in your life?

I encourage you to make this a habit that can transform your life. You see, this technique will help you to control and discipline your emotions, not to eliminate them. Our emotions are like a river. Their power can be dammed up and released in the right channels under your control and direction. You can cause them to flow in a direction of your choosing toward the attainment of your goals and definite major purpose.

The Happiness of Applied Faith

To put these principles into practice does require faith. Undoubtedly, you have encountered and been taught or are familiar with many different definitions of faith, and some of them have appealed to you more than others. There are as many different definitions of faith as there are persons who have seriously contemplated the great universe in which we find ourselves and who have arrived at an explanation of the elements of our environment which gives them the courage to face life with chin up, eyes bright, and a smile on their faces. The kind of faith that I am talking about is applied faith: the kind of faith that you can put into daily practice without regard to any form of theology or religion. You should use your own mind and reach your own conclusions on this profound subject.

Two of my favorite quotes on the subject are as follows: "The sun, the moon, the stars, the seas, the hills, and the plains. Are not these, O Soul, The Vision of Him Who reigns?" – Lord Tennyson. The other came from a movie that our family used to watch when the kids were little. It is called "Contact." Jodie Foster plays a woman named Ellie. As a young person, the character Ellie was really interested in science and the planets and the stars. Scientists often do wrestle with the idea of faith and infinite intelligence. Her Dad had gotten her a telescope and was encouraging her in her pursuit of science and the study of planets and the celestial bodies in the heavens. I remember thinking many times about the dialogue between her and her Dad. Young Ellie asked her Dad, "Do you think there's people on other planets?" Her Dad replied, "I don't know, Sparks. But I guess I'd say if it is just us ... seems like an awful waste of space."

The Happiness of Perspective

I am sharing all of this with you out of my own struggle. During the recent Great Recession, I experienced considerable economic downturn. My businesses suffered and I was faced with great adversity and defeat. So, as much as it embarrasses me to admit it, I was miserable and unhappy and probably one of the most ungrateful people on the planet. It's a true story that when I realized how miserable and awful my attitude was, I started working to change it and I actually had to push my face cheeks up to smile. It had been so long that the muscles no longer worked properly. And although I did not suffer nearly as some others did – I didn't stop to give thanks that I still had my family and I never lost my home. I did lose a lot of money and some of my pride, but it is out of that time period that I created the real estate company and, like a phoenix rising from the ashes, I was able to recreate my professional world. I am so thankful to my coaches and mentors during that time. They held me accountable and guided me back toward victory. During that time, I learned to plant my garden. You see, I needed to study natural law and I needed to learn patience. In fact, I learned to grow plants from seed. And I studied and worked on my personal development every single day. I listened to every recorded message I could find on Dr. Hill's principles in *Think and Grow Rich*.

Happiness and Cultivating Gratitude

I listened to *The Secret*. During *The Secret*, one of my favorite segments involves a man who gave a friend a gratitude rock. I encourage you to watch it – you can find it on Netflix. Anyways, I live on the bay and I began to walk along the shoreline and I began to notice all the rocks that washed up on the beach. I began to gather them and then I began to polish them. I googled "rock polishing." I bought polishers and began turning those rough, ugly pieces of garbage into treasure. Then I began to give away my own gratitude rocks. If we get an opportunity to meet, I will gladly provide you with a bag of beautiful Virginia hand-polished gratitude rocks.

I think that period of my life has taught me more than any other time. It was out of those great struggles that I am writing to help you today. I also learned the daily practice of gratitude meditation. My wife and I spend the first ten minutes of every morning in gratitude meditation. If you send me an email, I will be glad to email you the YouTube link to the gratitude practice.

You see, some of the greatest happiness in life is born out of our deepest sorrows – and to find real and lasting happiness, find a way to give back. Find the joy in serving others – I did.

The Happiness of Discovery

But, maybe you are having difficulty with all these thoughts of happiness and you just can't figure out why or what's going on with you. You want to feel good and take part in all these happy emotions you are reading on the page, but it just isn't happening for you. Please know that you aren't crazy and you aren't alone. There is science to back up what you are experiencing. It's most likely the fear of success. You see, it's possible that you were conditioned in early childhood to believe that success equates to risk. Maybe you identify with the saying, "Don't get your hopes up." Or worse, "You don't deserve…." That type of thinking layers in threats of disappointment. Our subconscious goes to work trying to protect ourselves. It often shows up because we were told we did not measure up or weren't good enough in some way or on some level. Like we talked about earlier, our thoughts then are created around this habitual pattern of thinking and they just kick into repetition and reinforcement of what we already think. That leads us to the conclusion that we do not deserve success. In fact, even those who were not abused in any way associate success with negative consequences, such as competition, or jealousy and envy, and even greed. That is why the gratitude meditation and exercises are so helpful to the soul and powerful in transformation of thoughts and feeling patterns. In order to ferret out the possibility that this may be the cause of difficulties for you, here's an easy exercise:

Think about an event from your past when you were successful and excited. Using your imagination, replay that event in your mind. Now notice what you were feeling and sensing in your memory. Stay with this visualization for five minutes. You can use a stopwatch, or your phone, as a timer to remind you when the exercise is complete. Journal what you experienced.

Now think about a recent overwhelming situation and think about what you were feeling and sensing. Now go back to visualizing your success story. Were the feelings and sensations the same? Journal what you discovered.

Now is the exciting step – by isolating that thought, you can now change it. By changing the thought, you change how you feel. By changing how you feel, you change how you act. By changing how you act, you change the results, which increases your overall happiness and leads to a better life.

Fred's Story

Some people naturally look at the glass as half full and some people simply look at the glass as half empty. It's just a natural disposition and a habitual way of thinking and establishing a certain worldview. Prior to working together, Fred had a fairly successful real estate practice, but he was like Eeyore in Winnie the Pooh, just had a basic melancholy disposition. When we started working together, we were able to channel the things that Fred was naturally good at – creating clients, generating revenue – and turn those thought processes into mental disciplines, which were designed to increase his overall happiness. Fred has experienced a ten times return in financial gain by establishing the systems we worked on together, but more importantly, Fred is now enjoying his family life, more in love with his wife, bought a new home which they planned and accomplished together, and is able to focus on his children's sporting events without seeing everything through a negative mental attitude. He looks happier, makes more money, and is a sincere joy to have in the office. It's been a true pleasure to watch Fred's transformation. It was quick and it was easy by implementing The Shaffer Way.

I will also share another hack that I use and I really find it very therapeutic to me, so I am happy to share. Simply google the song "Brave" by Sara Bareilles. Pull up the lyrics and turn it up – loud!

And sing this song at the top of your lungs. As a suggestion, you might want to find a place where no one else will hear you if you aren't a great singer. Ok, stop everything and google it – right now on YouTube. Let's listen to it. Honestly, I want to see you be Brave!

Here's another personal story – my wife recently became a Yoga Instructor. And through her example, I have learned a great love for the practice. During one of my yoga classes recently, the instructor invited the class to begin thinking about the things you love about yourself. Then, she instructed us to begin thinking about the things you don't love about yourself. And next, she really said something that made a profound impact on me – now, make both parts of yourself, the one you love and the one you don't, reach up and have them hold hands. At first, I gritted my teeth and it was especially funny when I shared the experience with my wife. She just smiled. Sheesh – yoga teachers! But my friend, please know – you are beautifully and wonderfully made and you deserve every happiness this world has to offer. And, today is the first day of the rest of your life – live it, love it, laugh, and hug someone you love – especially yourself.

And know that I am here for you! Would it bless you to receive a Virginia gratitude rock? If so, just email me at jarettshaffer@gmail.com. I have personally harvested them from the Chesapeake Bay and am happy to send one to you. I would love to hear from you!

Chapter Six:

Step Three – Antidotes

"Little Alice fell down the hole, bumped her head
and bruised her soul."
– Lewis Carroll, *Alice in Wonderland*

There are a number of insidious obstacles to personal freedom, which may include preconceived ideas, thoughts, social norms, cultural beliefs, and feelings that stand in our way and prevent us from experiencing transformation. And, it's very possible that right now you are feeling stuck, blocked, or hurt. Part of our system is to address and administer the antidotes that will relieve, prevent, and counteract areas that have held you captive, until now. Let me share a powerful true principle that I learned to illustrate this point.

Getting Unstuck

In many parts of Asia and Africa, people use a method for trapping monkeys. To make the trap, they hollow out a gourd, leaving an opening just large enough for the monkey to place its hand in the opening. Inside the gourd, the hunter places a sweet treat, nuts, bananas, or other tasty treats that appeal to monkeys. They place the gourd somewhere easy for the monkey to find and attach a vine. They then stake the vine to the ground somewhere out of sight. The unsuspecting monkey smells the treat and reaches in to grab the prize. However, the opening was just large enough for the monkey's hand to go inside, but too small for the clenched fist with the treat to pass back through. No matter how hard or how much the monkey yanks, he simply cannot escape as long as he tries to hang onto the treat.

Blocked

So maybe you have an intuitive sense that you are hanging on or a vague idea that something is keeping you from the freedom that you desire but you just can't quite pinpoint what it is. Just as we have visual blind spots when looking at the road through our car mirrors, we also have psychological blind spots – aspects of our personalities that are hidden from our view. Some things are so close to us we can't see them at all. We're driving along, and a car pulls up alongside us. Because of its very proximity, we don't see it until we have to make that last-second swerve. Such is the danger of being too close to anything. So how do you know what your blind spots are? One place that blind spots can be found is in strong reactions.

Hurting

An unusually strong negative or positive reaction or stance may suggest what Freud called reaction formation. Reaction formation involves unconsciously transforming an unacceptable or undesirable impulse into its opposite. For example, in Shakespeare's Hamlet, the phrase, "The lady doth protest too much." With this concept in mind – and being especially mindful to leave out any shame or self-judgment – just notice what you notice as we examine the basic fears. Nearly everyone in the world suffers from at least one of them and some people suffer from all of them. The other clue that will help us is when we seem to encounter the same problem, the same predicament, the same situation over and over again. And this time, instead of the same story we have told ourselves in the past, let's take a different path. Take out a pen and paper and jot down any of the following that are interfering with your current real estate production.

The Fear of Poverty

The first of the basic fears is the fear of poverty. The fear of poverty can be very destructive. Poverty brings a great deal of suffering and only those who have experienced it can understanding its full meaning. One of the symptoms of this fear is a lack of ambition. It manifests itself as accepting whatever life hands out without challenge. Another symptom is the failure to make decisions – relying upon others to make them instead – and then secretly resenting the impact and result of those decisions and then placing blame upon the decision maker. Another is making excuses for failures, offering alibis, and then envying and criticizing others' successes. Next is living beyond current economic means, being intemperate in personal habits and lacking self-control, then finding fault with everything and everyone. Another is being pessimistic and expecting failure instead of success. The most difficult to tackle is procrastination. It is a habit that must be broken to achieve lasting success.

The Fear of Criticism

The second is the fear of criticism. This is a basic fear of what people will say or think. It undermines self-reliance and creativity and can turn into an inferiority complex, resulting in people-pleasing to gain acceptance and even love. Often the most hurtful critics are our relatives. The mastery of this fear will lead to an increase in self-confidence.

The Fear of Ill Health

The third is the fear of ill health. Some of the symptoms include the drug store habit. Another is the habit of self-pity, playing sick because of feeling sorry for oneself. And a third is the habit of over-indulgence, in any area.

The Fear of the Loss of Love

The fourth basic fear is the fear of the loss of love. This fear, over time, causes blindness to new options and causes an aversion to risk as disappointments stack up. A gavel comes down in the emotional courtroom and only what is known is chosen to avoid an undetermined outcome. This type of fear is paralyzing and prevents the decision to take risks in exchange for rewards.

The Fear of Old Age

The fifth fear is the fear of old age and aging in general. It's great to know that some of the most successful men and women have developed their greatest achievements and done their best life's work after the age of 55 and some even after 60 and 70. In fact, Julia Child did not publish her first cookbook until she was 51, Laura Ingalls Wilder wrote her first novel at the age of 65 and Grandma Moses picked up her paint brush at 76. Those ladies didn't let the fear of old age rob them of success.

The Fear of the Loss of Liberty

The sixth fear is the fear of loss of liberty. We are blessed to live in a country in which we are promised life, liberty, and the pursuit of happiness. It is especially important to remember that in American history, when the United States has felt threatened, our response has often been repression. It is a crucial lesson to remember that our nation will not be made safer from the loss of civil liberties. Often this fear is expressed by restriction and the placement of greater constraints upon our freedom.

The Fear of Death

The seventh fear is the fear of death. Death is probably one of two things. It's either one long, eternal sleep or, if it isn't sleep, it's an experience on some plane far better than we have on this earth. In either event, there is nothing to fear because it's going to come anyway.

Fear is Simply a Gauge

As discussed earlier in the book, we are all hardwired to experience fear and there is no shame in experiencing it. Fear is designed to spur us into action. Fear is simply a gauge like those we have in a car. The gas gauge tells us how far we can go before we have to refuel. The speedometer is designed to tell us how fast we are going. It would be silly to get upset or angry or try to place blame or cast shame upon our car because it is reporting a state of facts. It provides that information so we can act upon it. The emotion of fear should be approached in a similar fashion. It's how we process those signals and what we do with the information that will predict the outcome – success or failure. It's not that any of this stuff is new, it is just that, perhaps for the first time, we are noticing what we are seeing. In the words of Sherlock Holmes, "I only see what you see, Doctor Watson, but I have trained myself to notice what I see."

The Antidote of Acceptance

One of the most important things to realize at this stage of the discoveries we are making is that we are in a vulnerable place of self-revelation. You must offer yourself all the tenderness and compassion you can muster. The worst thing you could do would be to realize, "Ouch, ok, that is a soft spot," and now promptly beat yourself over the head with a two-by-four for it. Just admitting and noticing that it is a soft spot is a very big step. We don't stop having emotions; instead we learn how to deal with ourselves and others compassionately. If we recognize that we are held sway by a destructive emotion or habit, it's like being caught in a riptide; if we struggle, we run the risk of drowning; if we let it take hold of us, we get swept out to sea; if we skillfully implement these systems and techniques, we can learn to swim at an angle to the current and we can make our way to the shore.

Jane's Story

Jane had a terrible childhood and it was the root cause of much suffering and a lifetime of self-sabotaging behaviors. The good side of this was that she was very driven to success. The bad part was that when she got success, achieved clients, and established systems, inevitably, she would experience a period of adversity and she would create drama, yell at clients, and basically, she just wasn't nice, because she was stuck, blocked, and hurting. She couldn't see that she was creating her own suffering and causing the circumstances to appear based upon her own patterns of behavior and thought processes which were deeply ingrained in her behaviors. By working together, she learned how to isolate the thought that was triggering the emotional response. By changing that thought, she was able to change her belief and that changed her emotion. By changing her emotion, she was able to change how she felt and it changed her results. She obtained the desired results because she no longer lit the proverbial stick of dynamite and stopped causing her own chaos. Once she was able to diagnose that she was causing her own pain, she was able to stop. Her business improved drastically because she is very skilled and has a lot of natural talents and drive. Within twelve months of working together, she feels like a new person.

The Antidote of Gratitude

I shared earlier how terribly ungrateful I had become and how it led me down my own rabbit hole. One of the great sorrows that I experienced during my time of self-imposed suffering was an estrangement from my son. His transition out of the home into adulthood was especially bumpy for our family and he and I fought daily. Eventually, all we did was argue with each other and neither of us looked forward to encountering the other person. And it really doesn't matter who did what. The fact is that unforgiveness and bitterness and refusing to let go is the equivalent of drinking rat poison and hoping the other person dies. Thankfully through the practice of these principles, he and I have repaired our relationship. It isn't perfect and we still have room to grow and fences to mend, but I look forward to hearing from him and I am proud of him. He's my only son. As I learned that hurting another then becomes an acting of hurting myself, I leaned into my gratitude practice and kept my mind focused on maintaining my own positive mental attitude. I also learned that our willingness to get to know our own destructive emotions can help us understand how others can easily feel those things too. It creates a greater sense of empathy and appreciation for humanity. When we are brave enough to step toward the person or thing we may have been afraid of, we may find they are remarkably human and remarkably like us. Our willingness to get to know our own destructive emotions can help us understand how others can easily feel these things too. We can then extend friendliness toward the joyful, offer compassion for those who are suffering, celebrate the good in others, and remain impartial to the faults and imperfections of others. Simply by refusing to perpetuate the norm, we change the norm.

The Antidote of Accurate Thinking

I learned a powerful principle from one of my coaches that can help in transitioning your thinking. Its known as OAR/ BED. Above the line thinking is the OAR: It consists of taking personal ownership, accountability, and responsibility. Thinking above the line helps us to become victorious in our thinking and our outcomes. Below the line thinking is BED, and consists of blame, excuses, and denial. The circumstances don't change – just your reaction to the circumstances based upon your thoughts and perceptions of what is taking place.

I am a Master Diver and my wife recently got certified. We were diving and it was one of her first twelve dives. My son is also certified and the three of us were in St. Thomas celebrating the holidays and having a wonderful trip, a beautiful day, and were excited about our two planned dives. We had completed our first dive, spent the required top time, and had submerged to about 60 feet. When diving you have to have a buddy for safety purposes and my wife is my dive buddy. We were swimming along, enjoying the coral and the fish, but something happened that was totally unexpected. My wife gave me the "no air" signal. Being a Master Diver, I thought for sure she didn't know what she was actually saying and her being so new to the sport, I thought it was simply a mistake. However, you plan for such emergencies before becoming certified. Before offering aid, it's especially important to make sure that you take care of yourself first. I checked my air supply, made sure I was good to go first – and this is an important point – only after protecting myself first did I share my regulator with her. You have to take care of yourself first before you can help others. We are taught as Master Divers that you don't want to turn a situation into two drowning victims. So, after assessing my own situation first, I checked her regulator to see if maybe it was stuck, or to determine what might be happening. My son had noticed something was amiss as well and came over to offer aid if needed. When checking her regulator, she indeed didn't have any air. Then my son checked it to see if something was stuck. My wife and I were breathing off my tank and my son was checking the diagnostics of my wife's tank. We discovered the problem – her tank was out of air. Now as you can imagine, that was a high-risk situation. We then took the necessary safety stops and surfaced and returned to the dive boat. Once on the boat, we discovered the problem. My wife's tank had not gotten swapped out. Even though we had paid for the dive and it was the crew's responsibility to swap out the tanks, ultimately, it is the responsibility of the diver to do all the safety checks before diving. It was a powerful lesson to the three of us regarding personal responsibility and we were very grateful that nothing bad happened.

The fact is: every day we have choices about who we are becoming. It's human nature to blame others when things go wrong. My family and I could have pointed the finger at the dive operator, the company, the dive master or the crew, but by taking personal responsibility, not only did we all become better divers, we viewed the situation accurately. It truly is a diver's responsibility to ensure the equipment is functioning correctly and the reason for the system of having a dive buddy is to avoid accidents and mishaps. Every day, we get to choose the system for our outlook and our mindset. It might seem counter intuitive but, it's the habit of taking personal responsibility that reduces stress and brings inner peace of mind.

The Antidote of Improvement

Now you have the basic framework to evaluate your real estate business to see if any of the seven basic fears are present and you have the antidotes to relieve, prevent, and counteract any area you discovered could use some improvement. If you haven't been getting the results you hoped for with your real estate career, you can change your outcomes by implementing these steps to health, wealth, and personal happiness. "Whatever the mind of man can conceive and believe, the mind of man can achieve!" – Napoleon Hill

Want to know more about antidotes? Have questions about implementation? I am here to help! Email me at jarettshaffer@gmail.com with your questions or comments. I would love to hear from you!

Chapter Seven:

Step Four - Focus

"If everybody minded their own business, the world would go around a great deal faster than it does."
– Lewis Carroll, *Alice in Wonderland*

I n Chapter Seven, we are going to examine your real estate business and bring it into very clear focus so you can begin to launch your new and improved real estate career into action with zest, energy, and renewed passion. But first, we need to examine your gifts and skills.

Focus on Specialty

Many, many years ago, there was once a sword crafter, and he was known worldwide by his reputation for creating these swords that were genius level. People revered this man. He was the master craftsperson of sword people. He was best in the world at what he did.

One day there was a great king, and the great king had heard about this sword crafter, and he said, "I must meet this man." So, the king's people went out and found this sword crafter in a very small village, and they brought the sword crafter to meet the king. The sword crafter came in and he was very humble and he was very gentle. The king, in return, was also very gracious and welcoming.

Then the king asked the sword crafter his favorite question when he would meet a master. He said, "Sword crafter, what is the secret to your extraordinary excellence at what you do?" The sword crafter said, "Well it's very simple, King." He said, "Ever since I was a young child, I was exposed to the craft of making swords." And he said, "I fell in love with it. It didn't only speak to my head and my logic, it spoke to me at the most deep and soulful level. It spoke to my heart." He said, "When I was a young child, I made a decision that I would be the master sword crafter." So he said, "As I grew up, I read books on sword crafting, and if something did not relate to sword crafting, if it did not have the word sword in it, if it did not look like a sword, if it had nothing to do with the art of sword crafting, I did not spend my time with it. That is the secret of my mastery."

The Focus of Specialized Knowledge

Well, that parable describes how to become the best in your chosen occupation. In many ways, it's the secret of being an expert in specialized knowledge in the real estate field. And, based upon the Definite Life Plan you created for yourself in the Systems Chapter, it's necessary to specialize in a particular area to obtain the best results possible. Specialization is defined as the process of concentrating on and becoming an expert in a particular subject or skill. And if you want to gain the greatest success possible in the real estate field, you need to make your focus small. I realize that may sound counterintuitive but it's not. Laser-like focus allows you to concentrate on your greatest strengths and will empower you to get the greatest rewards.

The problem is, you have probably heard all your life to avoid putting all your eggs in one basket. You have also been told the troubles with a one-track mind, but that is precisely how you should think. Otherwise, you will be a jack of real estate trades and a master of none. Focus all your attention in one particular area and you will glean the greatest results. Out of passion comes progress. Controlled attention is organized mind power. If you fix your mind with determination upon your goal, and become a specialist in your area of expertise, you are sure to hit the target of real estate success.

You have to prepare your real estate crop for success and get ready to plant a field that in due season will be harvested for great reward. When putting these practices into action, you will experience the law of increasing returns by planting, investing, and re-investing in yourself. You are the very best investment you could make because you are marketing personal service. Every competent farmer understands and makes use of the law of increasing returns. He puts this law into operation in the following manner: First, he selects the soil that is appropriate for the crop that he expects it to yield. Second, he then prepares this soil by plowing and harrowing and perhaps by fertilization, so it will be favorable to the seed he plants. Third, he plants seed that has been carefully selected for soundness, knowing that poor seed cannot yield a bountiful crop. Fourth, he then gives nature a chance to compensate him for his labor through an appropriate period of time. He does not sow the seed one day and expect to reap a harvest the next.

Marketing personal services effectively involves this same principle. Prepare carefully the soil in which you intend to plant the seed of service by selecting the clients you desire. Then, cultivates that soil and prepare it through conduct that is harmonious and cooperative. Plant in the soil the finest seed of service and be sure to plan an abundance of that seed, as not all seed will germinate and grow. After the seed has been sown, do not become impatient if you do not reap your reward immediately. Give the seed time to germinate. Keep working your plan – don't quit.

Master Salesmanship is based upon absolute faith in what one is offering for sale. Mastery of your subject matter will give you the necessary faith in yourself and confidence to win the clients you desire to obtain.

Focus on Being a Specialist

When you contemplate what you love to do, what doesn't even feel like work – what types of real estate sales are they? What has given you the greatest return on your investment of time, money, and effort? When you think back over your real estate career, when did you have the most synergy and energy for the work that you were doing? What actions were you taking every day? When did you experience the highest profit margin? Those two things might be different. This is a good time to go back and examine your values, passion, and purpose to ensure that you are selecting the right type of real estate sales to focus on. We are looking for patterns here so we can put together a really solid plan and turn you into a real estate specialist. We are looking for the type of sales that you are best at, that you can brand as your own special niche and shine as a real estate superstar.

Jack's Story

When Jack and I started working together, it was quickly obvious that Jack had become a jack of all trades and a master of none. He diversified to the point that he was spread so thin that he was causing his own difficulty in maintaining a constant stream of steady business. He had a database that was a mile wide and an inch deep. We started working together and began to narrow his focus, find out what he truly loved to do – which is working with sellers – and help him set up systems designed to generate a constant steady stream of listings. He has experienced a 33% increase in overall revenue in nine months of working together and applying the focusing techniques he learned in coaching. He is diligently applying the principles and experiencing the desired results. He learned to focus his efforts and success followed!

Focus on Working with Sellers

These are signs that you could be a specialist in working with sellers. Do you love to analyze data, prepare comparable market analyses, and predict time on the market? Do you love to collaborate with homeowners and strategize what marketing techniques and action plans you can put into place to sell homes more quickly than others? Do you love to concentrate on selling certain types of homes in certain price points? Are you better at selling corporate relocation properties, short sales, move-up sellers, second homes, luxury homes, coastal homes, military relocation, fixer-uppers, high-end properties, mid-range homes, condominiums, townhomes, single family homes, rural properties, lots and land, farms, homes in subdivisions, homes in the country with farms, new construction, rehabilitated properties, investment properties, multi-family units, duplexes? Are you good at offering repair suggestions, staging advice, pricing strategies, incentives, bonuses, open houses, Facebook, LinkedIn, Twitter, Instagram, Pinterest and other social media marketing strategies? How quickly do the homes you list sell? How are you in comparison to your competition? Are you better, for example, at listing homes on the water or the typical three to four-bedroom, 2.5 bath single family homes? Have you developed the right negotiation skills complete with the ability to listen intently to your clients' wants and needs and to separate them accurately? Are you able to isolate exactly what the real objective is and help your client to attain it? Can you mirror back to them and help them to determine if what they are saying and what they are expecting are the same things and, if they are different, do you have the soft skills necessary to guide them toward the actual path they are seeking? Are you great at closing the sale, the negotiation, the deal, and obtaining the very best results for your clients? Do people sing your praises when it comes to real estate? If so, in what area?

Focus on Working with Buyers

Here's how to recognize a gift as a specialist in working with buyers. Do you have a knack for helping first-time buyers find the perfect home for themselves? Are you great at working with move-up buyers and multiple transactions? Are you great at helping buyers create a strategy for real estate as a retirement plan or helping parents find the right college property for their children? Are you great at locating vacation homes or finding that perfect profile of a property that buyers classify as their dream home? Are you great at working with military families, luxury home buyers, condominium shoppers, or those looking for a great deal or a fixer-upper that they are willing to put in sweat equity to turn into their dream home?

I have a questionnaire that I put together that can help you guide your buyer into selecting the right home for them. I would be glad to share it with you. At the end of the chapter, you will find my email.

Focus on Working with "For Sale by Owners"

You may be best as a specialist in serving former For Sale by Owners and homeowners who suffered with an expired listing. Are you fantastic at taking a sale that flopped and just didn't get the goal accomplished all the way to closing? Do you like coming in and salvaging the situation and helping the homeowner come to some very realistic conclusions on why their property just didn't sell the first time? Are you great at analyzing what happened and providing expert advice to help them make their dreams come true? Are you good at having the tough conversations and offering up excellent advice mixed with grace? Do you have an intuitive gift for knowing what works and what doesn't and outlining that in a skillfully balanced sales presentation sure to help these disheartened folks get the service they need and deserve?

Focus on Working with Investors

Consider these options to be a specialist in working with investors. Are you great at finding those properties that could be rehabilitated and bringing the greatest short-term return on investment for your clients? Do you find trends in areas that have the greatest potential for rejuvenation and revitalization? Do you have a knack for ferreting out and hearing about homes that are going on the market by your super-duper networking skills and community involvement? Do you love architecture or are you great at selecting areas which could benefit from multiplex apartment complexes? Are you a super sleuth at finding raw land and or tear down opportunities for builders and developers? Are you a whiz at hooking up real estate investment strategies with hard money lenders and offering those services and products to your clients? Are you great at creating spreadsheets and long-term return-on-investment strategies sure to gain massive real estate holdings for your clients to help them build their financial portfolios and wealth building real estate investment opportunities?

Focus on Working by Referral

See if your genius would be as a specialist in working by referral. Are you fantastic at and not the least bit shy about asking for referrals from your current clients? Do you have a trend of working in certain neighborhoods or certain areas? Are you good at farming neighborhoods, getting involved in community yard sales, food drives, walks, charities, sporting events, throwing client appreciation parties, delivering seasonal pop-by gifts and goodie baskets? How about posting homes for sale on military community shopping areas, malls, beauty salons, financial institutions, collaborating with estate attorneys, doctors, dentists, teachers, firemen, nurses, and other service providers?

Focus on Working with Property Management

If these are you, you could be outstanding as a specialist in Property Management. Are you fabulous at representing homeowners that want to keep their real estate as a long-term investment? Are you good at helping them select the right price to offer their home for rent, procuring tenants, negotiating leases and property management agreements, getting repairs completed, getting the rent paid on time, finding the best return-on-investment for your clients? Are you good at finding the right tenants to occupy those homes and keep your homeowners book of inventory filled?

Focus on Working with Commercial Real Estate

You could be a specialist in Commercial Real Estate. Do you have a skill for finding the most profitable areas in town to place the right types of business and are you able to negotiate long-term leases on behalf of your clients? Are you exceptional at working with high-rise, high-end commercial towers or better at working with strip malls and small industrial complexes? Are you good at finding tenants for warehouse properties or kiosks in malls and finding long-term land leases perfect for placing multi-use industrial and commercial use properties? Are you better at designing and creating complex commercial projects and working with urban renewal projects and targeted city rehabilitation areas? Are you good at working with governmental projects and coordinating long-term strategic development?

Focus on What You Love to Do

Now that you have considered which of the above have cultivated a passion in your heart and the type of real estate sales you desire to pursue, you need to match that up with its earning potential to see if they align with your wealth building objectives formulated earlier in the book. A great formula that can help you assess your realistic financial projections was developed by Dr. Napoleon Hill, the author of *Think and Grow Rich*. He created what is known as the QQMA Formula – Q+Q+MA=C. The Quality of service rendered plus the Quantity of service rendered plus the Mental Attitude in which it is rendered equals the Compensation you will earn.

So, as a recap, we have covered Step One – Systems, Step Two – Happiness, Step Three – Antidotes, and Step Four – Focus in The Shaffer Way. Next up, we will revisit the QQMA formula and other financial tools and tips in Step 5 – Finance, the ABCs of real estate math.

Have a question for me? I am here to help! I invite your comments and your questions. Shoot me an email at jarettshaffer@gmail.com. I look forward to hearing from you.

Chapter Eight:

Step Five – Finance

"Why, sometimes I've believed as many as six impossible things before breakfast."
– Lewis Carroll, *Alice in Wonderland*

kay, so you know how lots of people roll their eyes and tune out when someone introduces the subject of math? I promise – this chapter is fun and its chock full of songs, games, and tons of tricks of the trade. So stick with me, and let's get started with a great song to kick us off: It's the ABCs of Real Estate Math. Search Google for the ABC song by Michael Jackson, turn it up, and it's your playlist for this chapter … "ABC, It's easy as, 1 2 3, As simple as do re mi, ABC 123, you and me, ABC It's easy as, 1 2 3, you and me, yeah!"

Finance Can be Fun!

My wife and I decided it was time to increase our savvy in finance and investing. We had just finished reading *Rich Dad,*

Poor Dad by Robert Kiyosaki and we were discussing a fun way to learn and implement more strategies for wealth building. In his book, Robert talks about the game he invented, Cash Flow. You can find the game at richdad.com. It's easy to download and free, and I totally recommend it. It's a great tool for changing your thinking when it comes to real estate math, or any financial investing for that matter. Its greatest pros are: It's a free download and an online game that you can play on your phone. It's a board game, so it's very familiar and yet builds in a great deal of common sense when it comes to dealing with money. It introduces vocabulary that many people aren't familiar with as it comes to financial investments, tools, and terminology. It teaches you how to read a balance sheet, how to evaluate expenses and investments, and how to make financial decisions quickly. In fact, while I can't vouch for that as a fact, Mr. Kiyosaki claims that if you play the game at least 100 times, it will change how quickly and accurately you can analyze and assess investment opportunities.

See so far, we have had a song and had a board game and you are still breathing. Stick with me. Let's dive into some numbers together. Don't worry – I will be your dive buddy and it will be fun!

Financial Dashboard

Let's talk about some basics. You will need a real estate dashboard to keep track of your metrics. A financial dashboard is very similar in concept to a car dashboard. It has gauges designed to let you know how the status of your financial situation. Some of the key concepts include profit, revenue, expenses, gross revenue vs.net revenue, and key performance indicators. Gross revenue is the total that you earn in real estate commissions and sales before anything is deducted. For example, and to make it simple, let's say you sold 10 homes at $250,000.00 per property at 3% commission per unit. The gross commission would be $75,000.00. That is, $250,000.00 x 3% = $7,500.00 gross commission x 10 units = $75,000.00.

Your goals are going to be targeted on your profit. Profit is what you earn after expenses are taken out. So, you have revenue minus expenses equals profit. Profit is what you get to actually deposit in your household checkbook and tangible money that you can have to fund your lifestyle. The goal is to establish a targeted amount of money to have as household income. It won't be worth it if you earn a gross revenue of six figures, say $100,000.00 and spend $100,000.00 to get to that number. Many people make this mistake and don't take the time to balance revenue minus expenses. Profit is the actual amount of money they have earned as a return for their time, talent, and efforts.

We need to target the amount of money that you want to have as household income, but we need to evaluate what your expenses are going to be to get there. Expenses include your brokerage split with your company, your dues, your marketing and business expenses, taxes, your vehicle and gas, and other miscellaneous business expenses. You will need to take all of those expenses into account and budget appropriately to get to your final desired number.

A very important concept is to pay yourself first. Have you ever wondered why the government takes their portion first before it comes into your hands? It's because they know this principle well. You might consider this your "me" tax. Be sure to pay yourself first before investing more money into your business. To learn more about this excellent concept of wealth building and investment, I highly recommend a book called *The Richest Man in Babylon* by George S. Clason. It's an easy read, taught in story form, and filled with powerful financial principles.

Finance – The Value of Time

To get a better idea of how to understand the value of your time, we have devised the 8, 8, 8, and 8 System for time management. The first 8 hours are for sleep, 8 hours for real estate activities, 8 hours for recreation and spare time activities, planned out in 8 week increments of time. I don't recommend taking away the time necessary for rest and rejuvenation which belongs to sleep as your body will need the sleep, especially during this time of increased activity and growth. The second eight hours should be dedicated to your real estate business. To evaluate how you are currently doing in regards to the eight hours that you are dedicating to your real estate career, I have devised a worksheet, which will help to identify the current metrics in your business at this point. This will give you a point from which to assess your current return on investment for your time and effort. I call it the Value of Time in Sales.

Finance – The Value of Time in Sales

To calculate your value in your current sales system – begin by taking the last 12 months in income. How much did you earn in the last 12 months? Take that number and divide it by 2080 – that is your value per hour. How do you feel about that number? Is it more than you thought it would be? Is it less? Would you like to change it? By how much and by when? How much did you earn last month? Divide that number by 173.33 to get your value per hour. How do you feel about that number? Is it higher or lower than your annual value per hour?

Time is the one resource that we all have that cannot be replaced. And, we are all given the same 24 hours per day, we just choose to invest those hours differently. It's important to choose to use them wisely so we can get the maximum return on investment for our time, talent, and resources. With that in mind, look back at your calendar for the last 30 days and answer the following questions: Was every meeting I went to worth my value per hour? Were some meetings worth more than others?

Think of a meeting you had in the last week that will definitely drive your hourly wage higher. How can you schedule more meetings like that one?

Pick a meeting from the past week that will definitely drove your hourly value lower. What do you need to do differently to avoid scheduling those types of meetings in the future?

As you look at how you spent your non-appointment time over the past week, what activities are you doing that definitely drive up your hourly value? Which activities are driving it down? Which of the activities did you enjoy doing? Which activities did you wish you had avoided? What can you do this week to drive up your value per hour? What can you stop doing this week to avoid driving down your dollar figure per hour?

Vanessa's Story

Without having the financial discipline necessary and the correct measurement tools, Vanessa was losing an incredible amount of revenue, simply because she wasn't reviewing her numbers. She was discounting her commission, devaluing her services, paying for repairs, inspections, etc., simply because she hadn't learned the secrets of applying the correct valuations and metrics to her business. Within six months of working together,

Vanessa experienced a 25% increase in overall revenue just from analyzing her own results, building in the financial measurements and disciplines she learned in coaching, and treating her business like a business! She's off and running and now we are free to focus on some of the other steps in The Shaffer Way so she can increase her overall returns. She learned that real estate math is easy and fun – and you can too!

Finance – Increase Your Value Per Hour

There are two ways that you can increase your value/hour. You can increase your earnings or decrease your hours. If you can figure out a way to earn more while working fewer hours, that is great. But realistically, the best way to increase your value/hour is by treating every meeting, every appointment, every phone call, each hour at your desk, and every conversation as if you are actually spending your value/hour. Continually, ask yourself, "Is it worth it? Would I spend $___ for this meeting or phone conversation?" If not, why are you doing it?

Would having a mentor or a coach increase your chances for success? Do you think you could benefit from that type of accountability?

This is where the use of a Customer Relationship Management System can be exceptionally helpful for tracking the day's activities. The definition of key performance indicators is: a quantifiable measurement used to evaluate the success of an organization or employee in meeting objectives for performance. There are many useful and helpful customer relationship management systems. Some examples include Buffini's Referral Maker. It's a simple and easy-to-use system which easily tracks all your real estate activities and gives you an easy point of reference to schedule your appointments, and to track all your real estate activities. You could also use Top Producer; it's real estate software designed to also keep track of clients and real estate activities. The point is to write down what you are doing each day and keep track of it in an easy-to-use format so you can track your results.

Finance – The Value of Tracking and Metrics

And to begin, you can keep track of everything manually. In fact, in 2016, when my wife and I were in the process of changing our patterns of behavior and basically getting our life back on track, I was given a journal in my monthly box from Buffini and Company. I am proud to say that I wrote in my journal starting January 1, 2016 and documented my progress every single day and journaled my day's activities to gain the habit of becoming self-disciplined and changing my world.

That journal changed my world. I had the courage to do things differently because I was motivated to get a different result. My wish is that my journey and my story can help you make the necessary changes in your patterns of behavior as well. Please know that our strength grows out of our struggles and I am right there with you. I have not "arrived" and am not writing to you from a high, lofty, superior position – I am sharing my struggles in the hopes you will be motivated and encouraged to know that you can change too. It's my hope that by implementing The Shaffer Way, your work time will be mixed with passion, fun, and enthusiasm so that it will not feel like a chore, but something you look forward to.

Tracking your results manually can change your business and your life. Beginning manually can often be the best way to overcome procrastination due to a fear of technology or learning a new computer system. Change can be difficult, so if it's easier for you, just track your results manually. For example, simply jot your daily measures down on a piece of notebook paper or in a journal. Keep those manual results for eight weeks and you have developed a new habit. Then, if you find it more convenient and beneficial, move your metrics over to a computer-generated tracking system. If not, manual tracking works just great. The point is, find the easiest method for you and measure your metrics for best results.

The Finance of How Time Is Spent

Many people find a great divide in how they spend their eight hours of leisure time and this often separates the successful from the unsuccessful. So, let's examine some principles on those eight hours. This is a suggested guideline on how to account for the eight hours of leisure/recreational time.

- An hour for reflection and study: This is best accomplished while having your cup of coffee, along with journaling and quiet meditation followed by the normal morning routine of dressing and getting out the door.

- Two hours for family time, preparing lunches, having breakfast, and in the evening sharing meals together, reflecting on the day's activities and discussing the day's successes with one another for peaceful harmony and love.

- One hour dedicated to study in which you can concentrate on increasing your specialized knowledge – which in turn will help you to increase the rate of your dollar per hour.

- One hour specifically dedicated to the attainment of your definite life plan.

- Three hours devoted to general recreation through entertainment, hobbies, exercise, and physical and mental relaxation and community service.

This schedule can be followed for six days per week with one day dedicated to rest and relaxation and rejuvenation. "Start by doing what's necessary, then do what's possible, and suddenly you are doing the impossible." – St. Francis of Assisi

A Financial SWOT Analysis

Next, based upon what we have discovered in this chapter as to the use of our time, it's important to count the cost of how we spend our time as well as our money. We all have the exact same twenty-four hours a day. The only thing that separates the successful from the unsuccessful is how those hours get spent. With that in mind, go back over the value of time in sales, brainstorm by quickly writing down as many of the items as you discovered were strengths or weaknesses. Give yourself two minutes. Be sure not to criticize – just let all the ideas pour out of you and onto the page in each area. Once you have completed the exercise, go back over each list and keep only the top three in each category. What do you see to adjust in how you use your time?

Take courage and be brave – you got this!

Chapter Nine:

Step Six - Execution

*"Begin at the beginning," the King said, very gravely,
"and go on till you come to the end: then stop."*
– Lewis Carroll, *Alice in Wonderland*

Execution – Contacts

So, if I asked you what is the highest priority in real estate? I am likely to get an answer – closings, of course. That's where the rubber meets the road, how the dream becomes reality, and now that the work is done, it's time to put it to rest and move forward.

But there are no closings without clients and there are no clients without contacts. The mental image I want you to conjure up is a picture of a funnel. Entering the broad top are the contacts, your database of names, faces, phone numbers, and email addresses. Inside the funnel itself, the contacts become clients. And, squeezing through the pipe to the opening at the bottom of the funnel are closings. They trickle through one at a time. And, closings are wonderful – keys and kisses – the commission check is just frosting on the top of the proverbial cake.

But it doesn't take long for the exhilaration to subside. You pay some bills, sock away a little for the future, and then it's back to work looking for the next client. Where will they come from? How soon will they arrive? Then worry sets in and you think, "Will my next transaction be enough to cover my upcoming bills?"

There should not be anything conditional or circumstantial as to where your next client is coming from. You can't control how quickly your closings take place, but you can control the number of closings you create by deciding on how many clients you will create. It's sort of like the old saying, "You can lead a horse to water but can't make him drink." Drinking is up to the horse just as it is up to your clients whether they decide to buy that home you are showing them. If you've got a large stable, it's not going to frustrate or panic you if three animals in a row don't put their lips to water because you have plenty more horses lined up and ready to consider the opportunity.

So, you need a large enough database that you can cultivate so you don't have to constantly worry which one will turn into the next closing.

Execution – Clients

So, it's time to do another paradigm shift in thinking and reverse the order from closings to clients. The switch will truly be liberating. Instead of the number of closings hanging around your neck like an albatross, keeping you up at night, or transforming every human being you meet into a possible paycheck – that's no way to live – it's instead about meeting people, ascertaining their needs, finding out how you can serve them, and converting them into clients. It's a much more satisfying way to define your role and purpose as a real estate agent. It's a financially successful approach as well, because those you stay in relationship with will indeed turn into a real estate transaction at the closing table. Take care of the clients and the closings will take care of themselves.

So, let's delve deeper. What do we mean by contacts and how can they be transformed into clients? Let's start by defining what contacts aren't. They aren't every name you have ever encountered. Nor are they every person you've ever met or even friends of friends on Facebook. Think of it this way: You don't want something crazy and overwhelming like 5,000 contacts in your database. Trim it back to only people that you would want to invite to your home. Suddenly the number will become much more manageable and you can envision serving those people. Think of 100-200 people you would happily invite and with whom you could actually have a great conversation if they attended your party. With that, you have gone from viewing it as a contact list to an invitation list. See how much more personable and rewarding that viewpoint is?

Identify each of them as relationships. What you are looking for are people you can comfortably talk to about their real estate needs, present and future; people who will understand and appreciate when you offer to be their real estate advisor of choice. The best and most successful real estate practitioners think of and position themselves as real estate advisors who view themselves as the professionals they are. You choose one primary care doctor, one accountant, and one attorney. Why should anyone fail to have a real estate advisor – someone who can answer questions, provide advice, and, when the time comes, help to negotiate a successful real estate transaction?

Execution – The System for Contacting Your Database

This is where your new customer relationship management system gets to earn its keep. Using the laser-like focus you established in Step Four of The Shaffer System, and zeroing in on the type of real estate sales that is your newfound passion and of the greatest interest to you, write down as many names as you can think of – keeping in mind that you are looking for relationships, not just names. Don't get too restrictive at first; you can include someone you served with on jury duty for example, as long as you made a great connection with them. Your car repair shop owner, if you have something in common with him/her and you have found common ground to have a conversation about something besides cars, your accountant, your dentist, your attorney, your florist, someone in your book club, your financial advisor, your insurance agent, your hair stylist – all of those qualify if you have shared experiences and the ability to carry on meaningful conversation. For these purposes, those contacts qualify as relationships and can go into your new and improved database of relationships.

Step two, reconnect. Making breezy phone calls works fine, your goal is simply to greet your contacts and find out what's new in their lives. Don't talk real estate at all, simply ask how they are doing and if they ask about real estate, keep it brief. It's OK to share that you are refocusing your business or that you have learned a new and improved system – yeah! You don't want them to feel as if the only reason you reconnected was to make money off them; it will cheapen the contact and defeat the purpose of the call. Instead, simply express excitement about what they are doing and what they are up to and leave it at that – and do what every good sales person does, steer the conversation back to him/her. As the best sales people know, the favorite thing for a client to hear coming off their professional's lips is something about the client's favorite subject: him/herself.

Step three, make a second call a week or two later. Since you have your dashboard, it should be easy to pull up the list each day of who you should be making contact with that day and document the interaction. Tell your contact you're just following up to see if he or she knows anyone who may be buying or selling property in the near future. If they do, you just found a client! If not, take the opportunity to say a few words about how you run your business. Tell them that client care is your number one priority and that you are trying to provide one stop shopping for a relatively small group of people in your community who desire top-notch and continuing service in all matters property-related. If they need information on available properties, valuations, repairs, refinancing, remodeling, investing, or anything else, ask them to please be sure to reach out to you first and to be sure to share the service you are offering to their friends, co-workers, and neighbors. Be sure to let them know that you'd like to be the first call they make if they need any real-estate-related information.

Step Four, categorize them as hot, warm, or cold to prioritize them for follow up and contact purposes. If they are ready, willing, and able to purchase or sell property, they are a hot client and immediate action needs to take place to best serve them. If they possess two of those categories, they are a warm client, and any of them that exhibit only one of the qualifications will currently be known as a cold client for the purposes of this week's activities. Just be sure to remember that clients can switch temperatures very quickly, very slowly, or not at all. Therein lies the art of real estate sales – you've got to be aware enough and systematic enough to be in regular contact to track their life changes. For example, do they have newborn children, or have all the kids flown the nest? Has there been a job change or a divorce? Do they have an aging parent that will make their housing needs change soon, or young adults that are planning to go off to college, making the change of residences a desirable and appealing alternative? Offer to be there for them during all of these transitions, answering questions, exploring options, and finding the appropriate solutions with which to serve them best.

Execution – World Class Service

It's uniquely important to have that mind shift to thinking of yourself as a concierge. You want to be seen as a problem solver, advice giver, and service provider. You want to be the real estate brain for your clients, not just once or twice in a lifetime, but on a somewhat regular basis. People want the kind of information that a real estate agent has access to – they just don't want to encounter a pushy sales person. If you set yourself as a service provider, the attitude and mindset of the client completely changes. You know what's happening in the market, what's selling, what's not, and what sort of investment opportunities may be developing. You also have your finger on the banking industry and keep them apprised of current interest rates and loan programs that are becoming available. If people are moving into the area, you know where to direct them for recreation, where the health clubs are, the libraries, and restaurants, where the schools and shopping and beaches are located. You start to position yourself as their real estate resource and turn into a valuable contact, not a salesperson to be avoided.

You need to have a script and a systematic approach to time and touch contact points in your time management system. In my coaching with my agents, I teach them how to follow up, ask the right questions at the right times, how to find out if your contact is interested, and whether your client's status has warmed up or cooled off. There is absolutely nothing wrong with having a structure for your calls – you don't have to fly by the seat of your pants, which is not recommended.

Execution – Getting Referrals

Step Five, getting referrals. Here are three truths about referrals.

One, each referral received represents an agent's energy saved. No cold calling or internet prospecting. You have received the ultimate compliment, someone's name and telephone number and insider information on whether they are ready, willing and able to buy.

Two, each referral holds out the possibility of more referrals as long as the service they have received has been exceptional and you have remained in contact.

And three – this last truth is vitally important and often overlooked – referrals are sought too late and taken too lightly. Most agents tend to wait to ask for referrals until at the closing table. That is the wrong timing altogether. The client has already begun to cool off, their excitement has dimmed, and although grateful, they are glad to stop talking real estate for the time being. So, our system calls for the creation of a mutual set of expectations, both the agent to the client and the client to the agent. That's right, it's a two-way street in our system.

Here's what we advocate as the agent's responsibilities: answer calls quickly, provide information requested, bring to client buying or selling opportunities, inform clients of legalities including disclosure rules, complete paperwork quickly and accurately, and deliver ethical caring and individualized service. The agent then has an expectation of the client which includes: fully informing the agent of wants, needs, and financial constraints, responding quickly to agent communications, offering exclusivity to the agent and providing referrals.

Providing referrals should be a key condition of the relationship. A solid expectation that you should declare to each and every client that you are currently working with is an expectation of receiving two referrals from them before their closing is complete. They will be the most excited while you are working with them and talking at every opportunity about their real estate transaction and your excellent and outstanding service. This is the perfect time to get additional business and it's the most cost effective and predictable way of working with clients and planning for the next real estate transaction. You should be sure to let your clients know why it's in their best interest, i.e., what's in it for them to give you referrals.

Now most will be so excited that they will be delighted to give you referrals but for the shy or more reserved client, be sure to let them know that the average real estate agent is spending 80 percent of their time just finding and securing clients. If they provide you with referrals, you can spend all your time serving them. So you can put the question on the table to your client, "Would you rather have me spend 80% of my time into advising and serving you and successfully closing your transaction or looking for the next set of clients?" And the referral you are looking for is an introduction, not just a name and number.

Here's where the mind shift happens: A referral is not a favor offered as a reward to a real estate agent; it's a necessary condition of the working relationship and sure to guarantee them the concierge service they are looking to experience. The script for having this conversation goes like this, "My real estate business is set up like a practice and I limit the number of clients I work with, much like a doctor or accountant does. I want to be the person they come to when they have a property related question or problem and I want to dedicate my time and attention to help them make all real estate related decisions, not just those decisions which turn into contracts. In exchange, my clients offer me referrals, but without those introductions, I simply can't put the time into providing the concierge level service that I offer."

Less usually is more – don't be greedy. Too many introductions turn into a time management nightmare. Tracking and following up at the right time is the key ingredient to success.

Kayley's Story

When Kayley and I started working together, she had never stopped to analyze where she obtained her business. She was already producing several million dollars in real estate sales on an annual basis, but her execution was low in producing a steady stream of repeat and referral basis. By analyzing her successful real estate career of over twelve years, we were able to pinpoint the source of her business, tap into systems designed to stay in touch, and empower her to ask for business while working with her clients, instead of making the mistake of waiting until the closing table to ask for referrals. She learned the excitement of the buyers and sellers was at its peak when working on finding that home or selling their property. By doing a better job of implementation, strategizing, and executing based on the established systems, Kayley was able to double her business in the two years we have been working together. She has learned the value of execution and the power of consistency.

Execution – Lifetime Value of Clients

Step Six. Now that you have a steady book of real estate clientele that are being referred to you on a regular basis, you can categorize your clients according to their customer lifetime value (CLV). The customer lifetime value of a client is how much business he or she represents over a given period of time. Type one referrals are the prime ones, the ones you would never have won as clients without the help of a referring client. Type Two referrals are those whose business you would have won even without a referral but their value is in the money saved in not having to market to them. Make note that clients who bring you lots of listings or make serial purchases with you aren't necessarily great sources of referrals. What is important is to rank and prioritize clients based upon their customer lifetime value.

Chapter Ten:

Step Seven – Rewards

Morpheus: "This is your last chance. After this, there is no turning back. You take the blue pill – the story ends, you wake up in your bed, and believe whatever you want to believe. You take the red pill – you stay in Wonderland and I show you how deep the rabbit-hole goes."
– The Matrix

My guess is that you have stuck with me throughout the book because something in your soul knows that your dream come true is right around the corner. And as you have devoured these chapters, the light has grown brighter and the hope has become palpable, you can feel it, you can taste it, you can smell it, and you can see it. I know that I can visualize you and I am cheering you on – you can do it, you can do it, you can do it!!! You and I have been on a journey together and I hope as I have shared my own personal struggles, they have helped you feel empowered and like you can do it too. At this very moment, you are standing at a crossroads and as we cover this last chapter together, at the end, you are going to have some choices to make. I would like to share one of my favorite poems with you, written by Robert Frost. It talks about this crossroads that you are standing at and the decisions ahead.

Two roads diverged in a yellow wood,
And sorry I could not travel both
And be one traveler, long I stood
And looked down one as far as I could
To where it bent in the undergrowth;
Then took the other, as just as fair,
And having perhaps the better claim,
Because it was grassy and wanted wear;
Though as for that the passing there
Had worn them really about the same,
And both that morning equally lay
In leaves no step had trodden black.
Oh, I kept the first for another day!
Yet knowing how way leads on to way,
I doubted if I should ever come back.
I shall be telling this with a sigh
Somewhere ages and ages hence:
Two roads diverged in a wood, and I –
I took the one less traveled by,

And that has made all the difference.

Unconscious Incompetence

The process of transformation that this system delivers takes place in four stages. Think of it like four stair steps that have to be ascended. The first step is unconscious incompetence. You have heard the saying, ignorance is bliss, but, you know, people say that tongue in cheek. You and I both know that ignorance is not bliss – it's denial and refusal to just plain accept things as they really are. Until that takes place, there is no way to move up to the next step.

The quote at the beginning of this chapter is from the movie "The Matrix," a great science fiction film from 1999 and it talks about the next step up. It's about a man named Thomas Anderson (also known as Neo) who lives an ordinary life. Anderson is a software techie by day and a computer hacker by night. At night, he sits alone at home by his monitor, waiting for a sign, a signal – from what or whom he doesn't know – until one night, a mysterious woman named Trinity seeks him out and introduces him to that faceless character he has been waiting for: Morpheus. A messiah of sorts, Morpheus presents Neo with the truth about his world by shedding light on the dark secrets that have troubled him for so long. It's a great analogy for where we are in this story, but you are the main character and only you can decide what comes next.

Conscious Incompetence

You can take the blue pill and this story ends – unconscious incompetence. In the movie, Neo is promised that if he takes the blue pill, the story is over, he wakes up in his bed with a basic bad feeling that things could have changed, but he goes along with his life and never is the wiser for the experience. But, that isn't really the case here. You are smack dab in the middle of conscious incompetence, in other words, you now know exactly where you are, you are awake to and have a full realization of exactly where you are stuck, what needs to change, and the fact that you have the power to make it happen and the system and steps laid out before you. So, what are the consequences of just giving up and quitting and deciding to put this book on the shelf, and pretending you never had this solution available?

Well, earlier in the book we talked about the envelope marked penalties. We are going to break that seal now and talk about what will happen next if you keep doing what you have been doing. What happens if you know what you could do to change and you decide not to? Unfortunately, things are going to get much worse. And now, with all this information firmly in place, if your real estate career isn't living up to your hopes, you can't blame anything or anyone, but yourself.

You will be up in the middle of the night and hearing the infomercials, because you can't sleep. You hear the paid for advertising guru promise a system for making a million dollars overnight using other people's money. They promise to microwave success, but the result is like trying to microwave a Thanksgiving turkey and, when you take it out of the oven, it's partially cooked, golden brown, but only on one side, because you only got half the recipe.

Then what sets in is disappointment. An undisciplined mind and unruly set of emotions further perpetuates the problem, resulting in many penalties, some of which include poverty and lack, laziness, envy, greed, vanity, fear and worry, frustration and doubt, cynicism, drifting without aim or purpose, irritability of mental attitude, the will to injure others, jealousy, dishonesty, and arrogance. Most of these symptoms result from a negative mental attitude and an unwillingness to go the extra mile, the attempt to get something for nothing, maintaining an entitled attitude, clinging to platitudes and self-righteousness – which is cloaked in deception and pride. Andrew Carnegie is quoted as saying, "There are two types of men who never amount to anything. One is the fellow who never does anything except that which he is told to do. The other is the fellow who cannot do even that which he is told to do. The man who gets ahead does the thing that should be done without being told to do it. But he doesn't stop there; he goes the extra mile by doing a great deal more than is expected or demanded of him."

Then there are those that try to take shortcuts. However, by refusing to implement all the necessary steps and trying to take shortcuts, a new problem appears. It's commonly known as the Doom Loop. The Doom Loop is another term for a vicious cycle, where an attempted solution just makes the situation worse because of the underlying system. For example, in a retail chain, same-store sales are falling. In response, management steps up the intensity of promotions. This has a temporary impact, but whenever the promotions end, sales return to free fall, faster than before. Management accelerates promotions again, until operations can't handle it and the supply chain breaks down.

The Doom Loop occurs when a superficial solution is chosen, without an understanding of the underlying problem. In the retail example, the real problem could be that the store has lost its differentiation in customers' eyes, and cluttering it up with price-based promotions just increases this perception. The short-term solution just made the fundamental problem worse.

The next step up is conscious competence. Do you remember when you first learned to drive and you had to think about everything – check your mirrors, adjust the rear-view mirror, press the gas pedal, press the brake, turn the turn signals on, where are the lights – and you had to think, OK, how do I turn on the windshield wipers? That is what it's like to arrive at conscious competence. You know what you know and you know how everything works and you have to be very diligent to make sure to stay in your lane, look before backing up, and basically talk yourself through the mechanics of driving.

Josie's Story

When Josie and I started working together, she was full of excitement and had absolutely no clue what she didn't know. It was delightful to fan the flame of her enthusiasm and carefully guide her through the process of setting up a systematic approach to her real estate business. She was a natural go-getter – but left to her own devices, quickly learned the typical real estate cycle of tons of business for three or four months and then nothing for the next three or four. We set about consciously focusing on establishing her real estate plan, following that with the Shaffer system of implementation and execution, and soon the financial and emotional rewards started rolling in the door. Now, she is quickly shifting gears and climbing the ladder of success. It's been a real joy to watch her progress and I am excited to tell you she did it in only nine months of working together. Now we are working on establishing permanent metrics so she can lock her systems into place and run an effective real estate business, along with having a successful family life. By implementing the steps she has received, her working hours are rapidly decreasing while her real estate sales are on the climb. It took intentionality to create her habits. That intentionality is the beginning of conscious competence.

Conscious Competence

Conscious competence is the stage where it's a cinch by the inch, and change takes place with playful consistency. Here's a fun and whimsical analogy to make my point: Picture an egg. Day after day, it sits there. No one pays attention to it. No one notices it. Certainly no one takes a picture of it or puts it on the cover of a celebrity-focused business magazine. Then one day, the shell cracks and out jumps a chicken. All of a sudden, the major magazines and newspapers jump on the story: "Stunning Turnaround at Egg!" and "The Chick Who Led the Breakthrough at Egg!"

From the outside, the story always reads like an overnight sensation – as if the egg had suddenly and radically altered itself into a chicken. Now picture the egg from the chicken's point of view. While the outside world was ignoring this seemingly dormant egg, the chicken within was evolving, growing, developing – changing. From the chicken's point of view, the moment of breakthrough, of cracking the egg, was simply one more step in a long chain of steps that had led to that moment. Granted, it was a big step – but it was hardly the radical transformation that it looked like from the outside. The Shaffer Way is simple and easy to execute. And, what follows is voila – your transformation. And you can absolutely start to make your dream come true your reality. It's not a fantasy or a child's fairy tale.

As I mentioned before, when my wife and I decided to take control of our personal health and improve our life span expectancy, it was almost 1,000 days ago. At first, when people asked me how we were doing, the question seemed to come up over and over again, "When are you going to step it up, increase the number of miles, change the goal?" You see, that's not the point; we weren't trying to work up to a marathon, we were trying to change our habits. It can be totally simple and really easy to implement. This system is designed in the same way. If you implement all the steps as outlined here, you will develop the necessary habits and character to have, be, and do anything that you set your mind to. You will be able to accomplish any goal, complete any task, and get from life anything you want. Not because you did some get rich quick scheme, but because you changed your mind.

Unconscious Competence

Nirvana happens when you climb all the steps and wind up at Unconscious Competence. Think of the last place you drove to. You didn't have to think about it at all, you just got in the car and almost like magic, you appeared at your destination with a vague recollection of how traffic was along the way. That is where we want to get your real estate business and your life to. The Rewards are yours and the choice is now. You came to this book knowing that you want success, you just need the courage to do something about it. And you have the courage in you, it's been there all along, you just need to rise up, take command and act, because you deserve every good thing this life has to offer.

And I am honored to be a part of your metamorphosis. Today is the first day of the rest of your life and every good and perfect gift can by yours, just decide, don't look back, and act, take the red pill, and call me in the morning.

Are you ready to get started? I am here to help! Just email me at jarettshaffer@gmail.com and we will schedule a strategy session, analyze where we need to start and begin your road to health, wealth, and personal happiness. I would love to hear from you!

Conclusion

We have come to the end of the book journey together but our work together doesn't have to end. I am here to help. You can absolutely implement the seven steps on your own and I will be in your corner cheering you on, but if you want to get to your goals faster and easier, I would love to be a part of your transformation. To get started, reach out to me at jarettshaffer@gmail.com so we can diagnose where you are at and come up with next steps and establish a plan together. I look forward to hearing from you!

Acknowledgments

A special "thank you" to Dr. Angela for helping me to channel my energy and create a book that will truly make a difference.

To the Morgan James Publishing team: Special thanks to David Hancock, CEO & Founder for believing in me and my message. To my Author Relations Manager, Bonnie Rauch, thanks for making the process seamless and easy. Many more thanks to everyone else, but especially Jim Howard, Bethany Marshall, and Nickcole Watkins.

I am grateful to my children for teaching me to stay one step ahead. They spurred me to keep growing and learning. That created a life pursuit of dedication to excellence and serving my community and my clients. I have learned so much from you both and I love you tremendously.

To my football coach who increased my determination to never give up.

To my Mom for loving me and always encouraging me when I was growing up. Her steadfast support kept me striving to achieve the best results.

To my Father for his unwavering love and his kind heart. I hope he enjoys reading this in Heaven.

To my clients who have believed in me. This book is dedicated to help you achieve all your hopes and dreams.

Here's to the journey!

About the Authors

J arett B. Shaffer is an entrepreneur, real estate investor, and Hampton Road's number one life coach and business strategist. Jarett is the founder, partner, and CEO of over 20 different companies including retail sales, commercial real estate endeavors, and real estate brokerage services. Jarett currently lives in Norfolk, VA with his wife, Susan.

Susan S. Shaffer has been a dynamic leader in the real estate, finance, and insurance industries for over thirty years. Susan is an author, motivational speaker, business coach, and certified yoga instructor. She currently resides with her husband of over thirty years in their beachfront home in Norfolk, Virginia.

Thank You

Thank you for reading Riches for Real Estate Agents. I have a thank you present to send you – a Virginia Gratitude Rock – to remind you that you can Have, Be, and Do Everything You Want! As a bonus, I will also email you the link to the Gratitude Meditation that my wife and I use every morning. Just email me at jarettshaffer@gmail.com.

And, if you want to turbo charge your way to Have, Be, and Do Everything you want – I will provide you with a free 20-minute call to help diagnose where you are on your journey – complete with recommendations and advice for next steps. To set up your complimentary call, email me at jarettshaffer@gmail.com and someone from my team will reach out to you and get you on my calendar.

You are a real estate rockstar! Here's to the journey.

Jarett Shaffer

CPSIA information can be obtained
at www.ICGtesting.com
Printed in the USA
JSHW021915280423
41009JS00002B/183

9 781642 793413